HELL'S KITCHEN FLEA MARKET

IMAGES OF NEW YORK'S FAMOUS OUTDOOR MARKET

BY

LAWRENCE VON KNORR
TAMMI KNORR

Cover image: *Mask* by Tammi Knorr

HELL'S KITCHEN FLEA MARKET: IMAGES OF NEW YORK'S FAMOUS OUTDOOR MARKET

Copyright © 2010, by Sunbury Press, Inc., Baron Productions, Inc. and Tammi Knorr.
Cover Copyright ©, 2010 by Sunbury Press, Inc. and Baron Productions, Inc.

All rights reserved, including the right to reproduce this book, or portions thereof, in any form or by any means, electronic or mechanical, including photocopying, recording, or by any information storage and retrieval system, without permission in writing from the publisher.

FIRST SUNBURY PRESS EDITION
Printed in the United States of America
November 2010

ISBN 978-1-934597-24-8

Published by:
Sunbury Press, Inc.
436 E Crestwood Dr
Camp Hill, PA   17011-1212

www.sunburypress.com

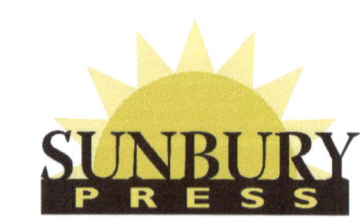

Camp Hill, Pennsylvania   USA

"There's no hypocrisy in Hell's Kitchen."

        Ethel Waters (1896-1977)

Dedication

To all New Yorkers – past, present, real, imagined, full-time or part-time and to Andy Warhol, who walked these streets in search of bargains and oddities.

Lawrence von Knorr
& Tammi Knorr

Introduction

Since the 1970's, a flea market has existed in the Hell's Kitchen neighborhood of New York City, at West 39th Street. It is home to oddities and curiosities from around the world, brought to this place by the myriad of New Yorkers and visitors who have come and gone from literally everywhere. Over the years, many celebrities have walked the market to pass the time and to find unusual keepsakes to add to their unique finds. While no celebrities were spotted on our recent visit (October, 2010), the variety and strangeness of the place was certainly up to expectations!

Contents

This book presents the photography of Tammi Knorr and the photography and digital fine art of Lawrence von Knorr.

Tammi Knorr is known for her unusual compositions of 'everyday things', discovering odd angles and details in her surroundings. She is an accomplished wedding, portrait and commercial photographer. This is Tammi's second book.

Lawrence von Knorr is a pioneer in Photo Impressionism – using computer software to turn his photographs into painterly creations. Lawrence's award-winning work has been shown in major cities across the country.

Following are photographs and digital enhancements of items and scenes from New York City's flea market at Hell's Kitchen. While most of the images retain their original or embellished colors, old fashioned black and white photography was also used to highlight the contrast in light, texture and form where advantageous.

All of these images are available in limited edition prints for purchase at the authors' gallery - West Shore Gallery in Wormleysburg, Pennsylvania. Please see http://www.westshoregallery.com for more information.

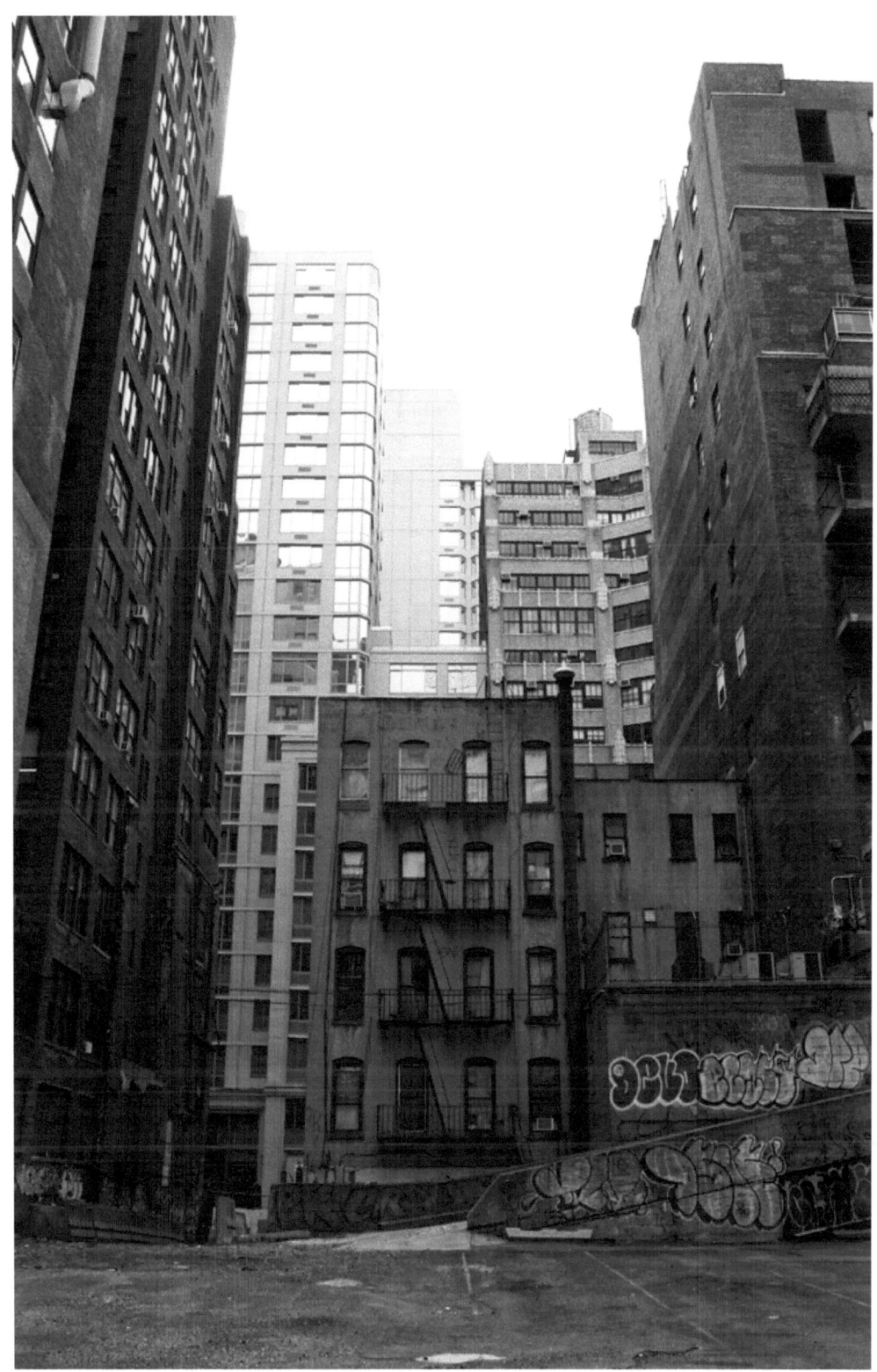

"Hell's Kitchen Tenement" by Lawrence von Knorr

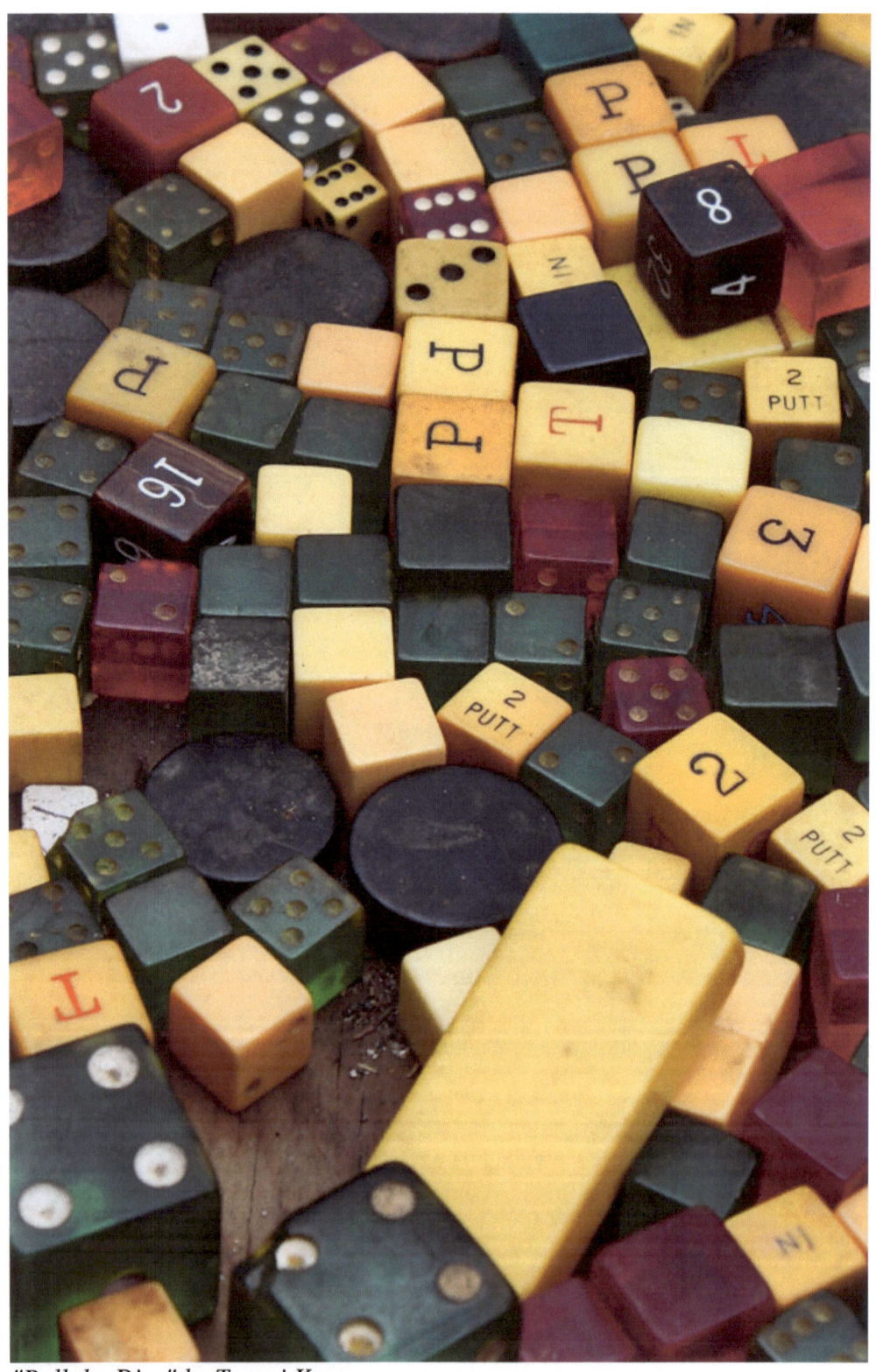

"Roll the Dice" by Tammi Knorr

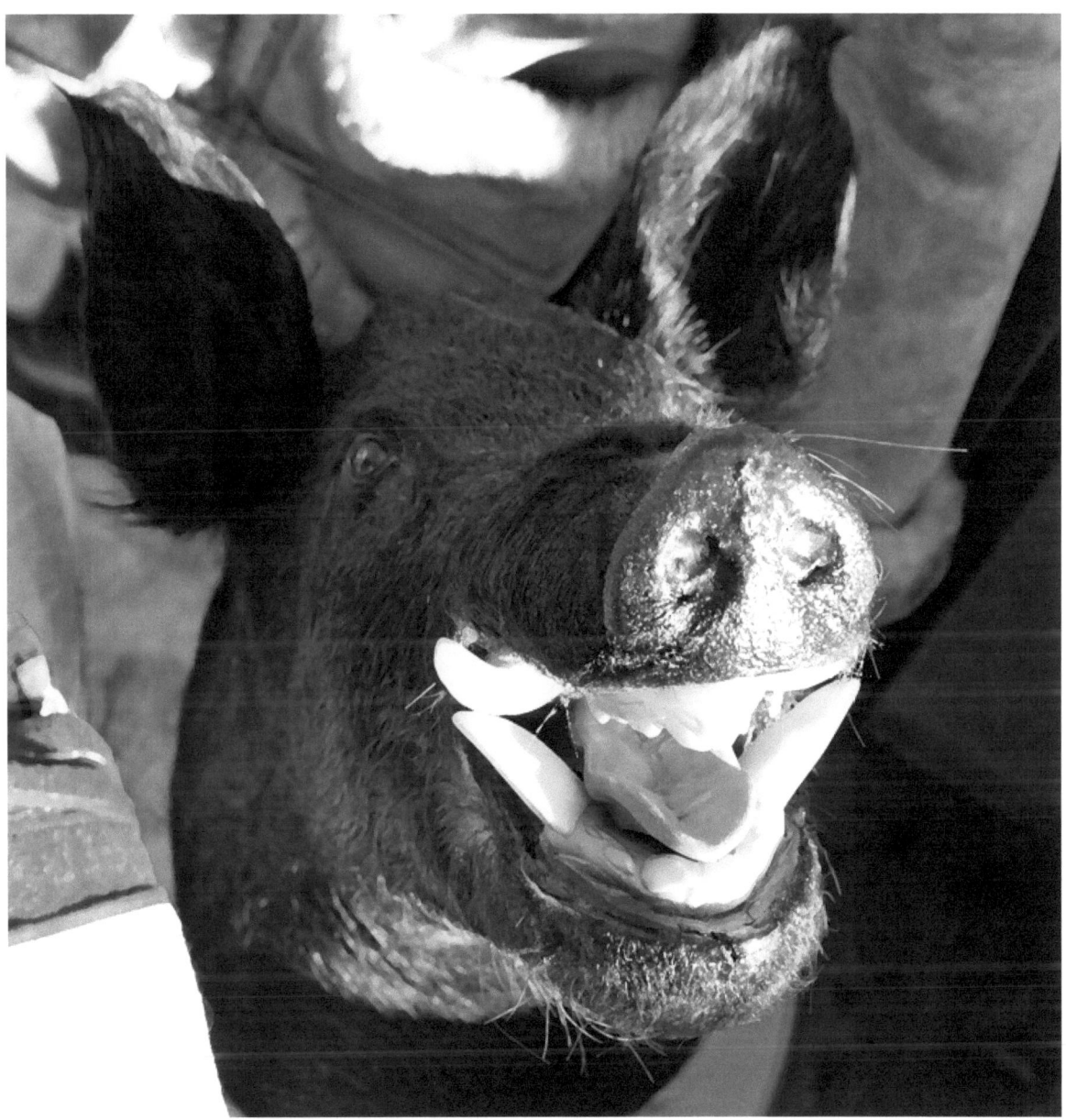

"Boar" by Lawrence von Knorr

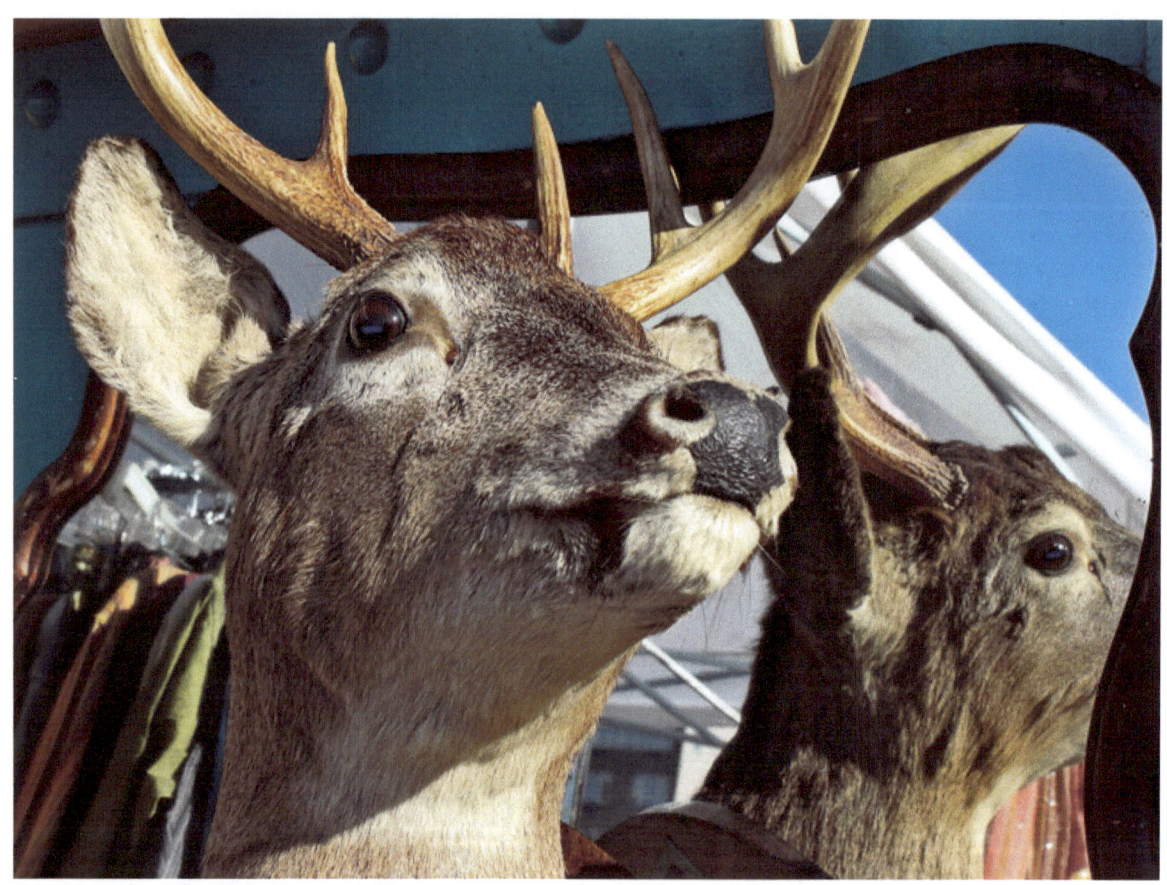
"A Dignified End" by Tammi Knorr

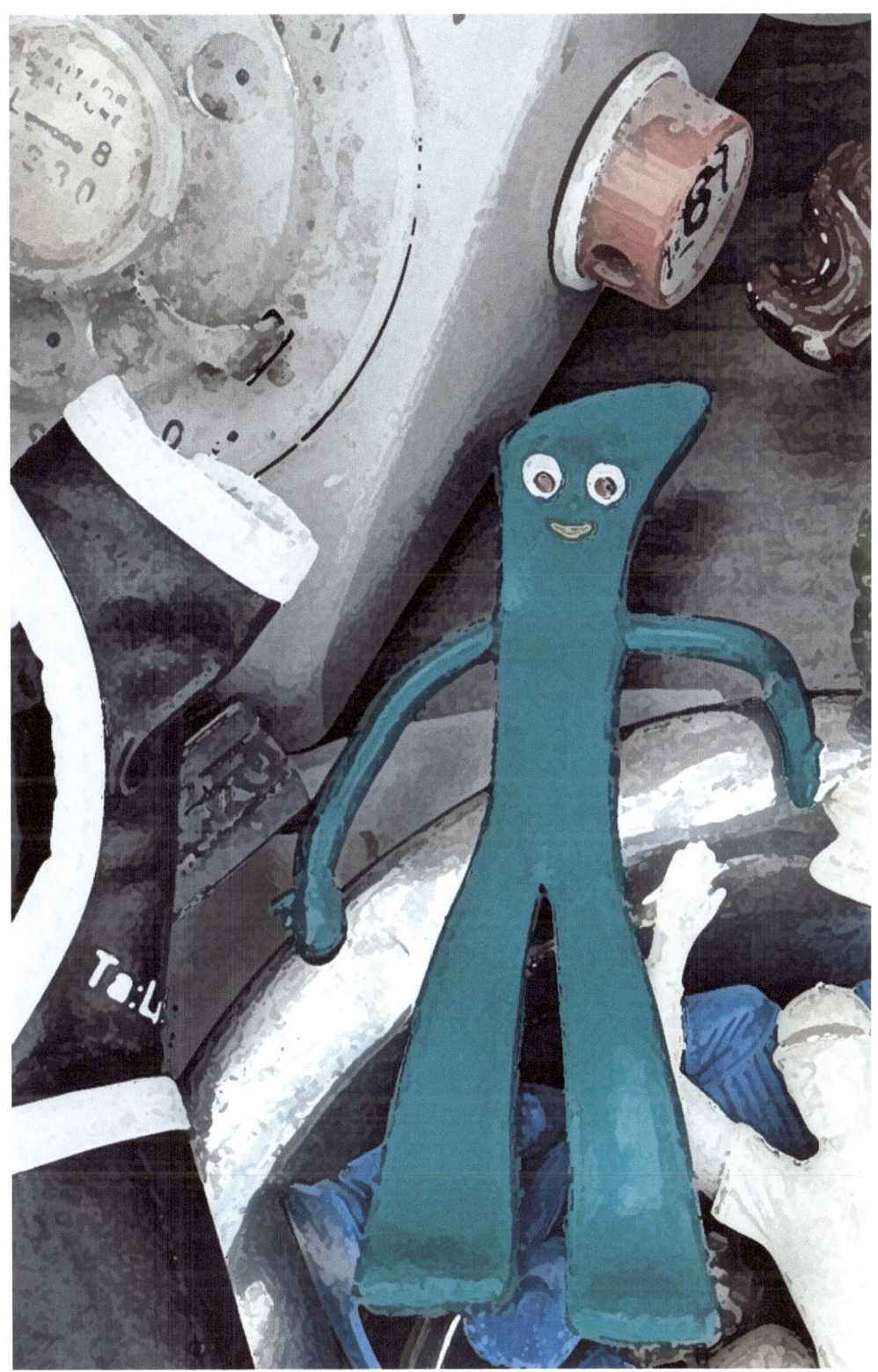

"Calling Gumby" by Lawrence von Knorr

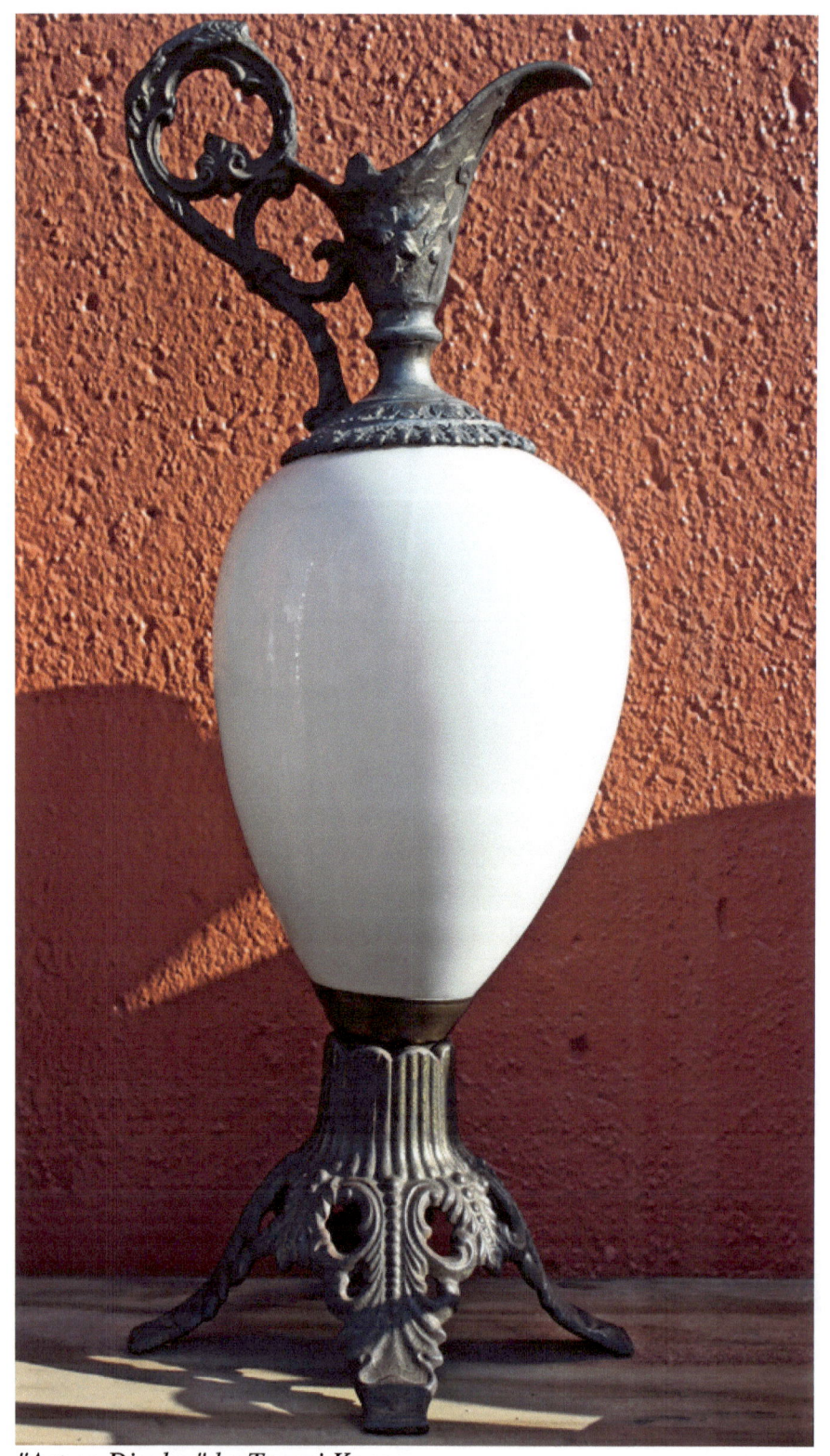
"Art on Display" by Tammi Knorr

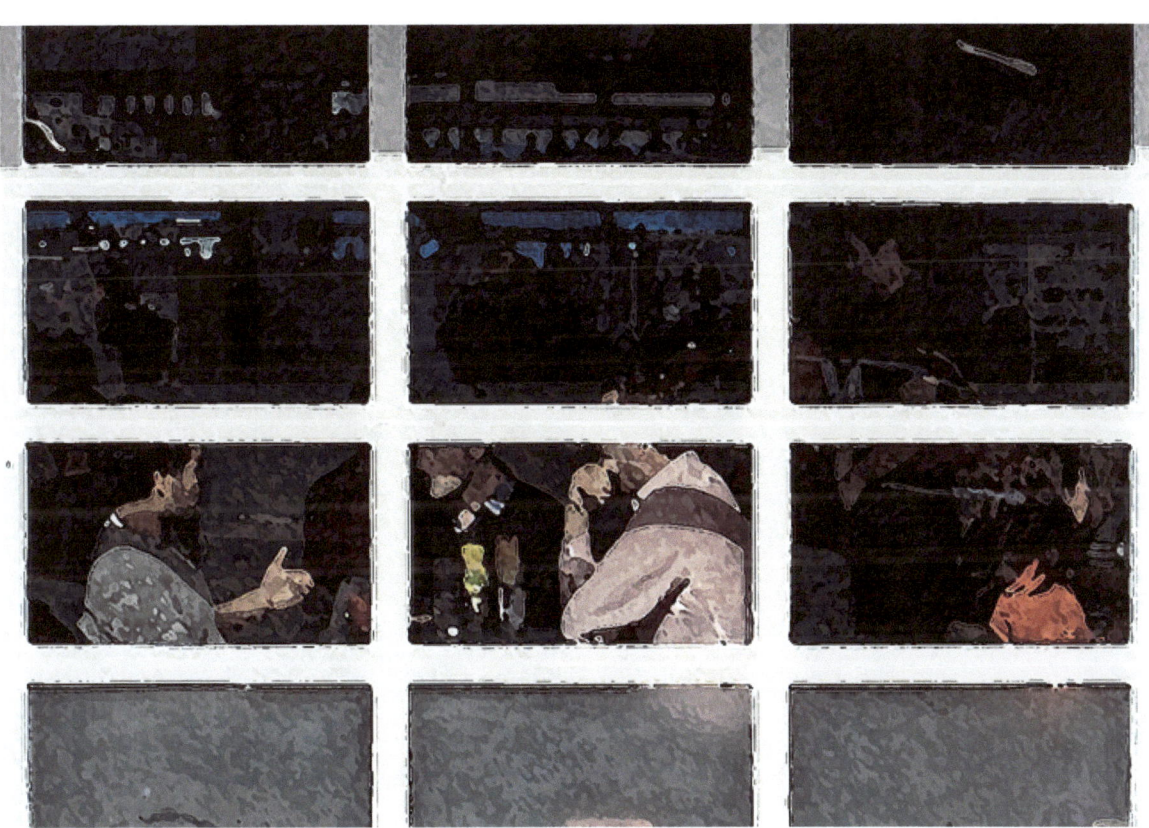

"Diners Through Windows" by Lawrence von Knorr

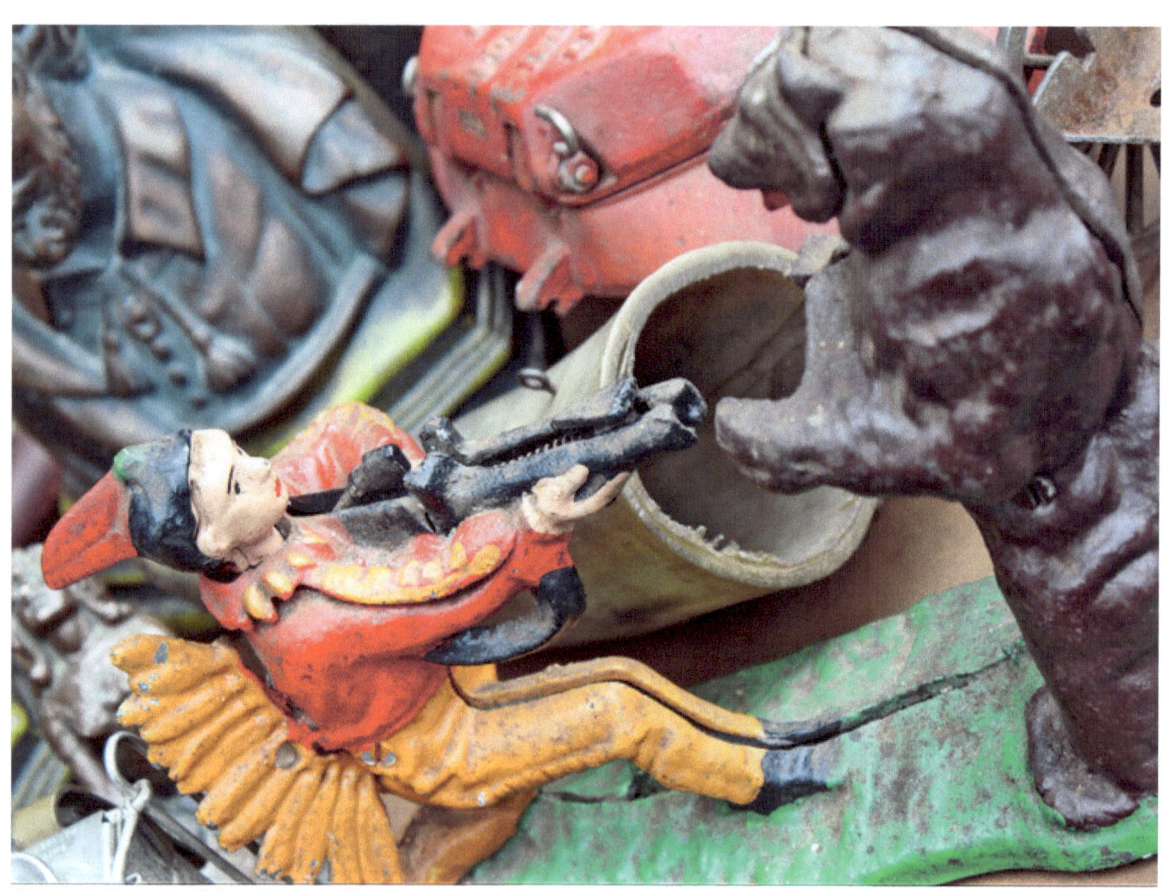
"Bear Hunting" by Tammi Knorr

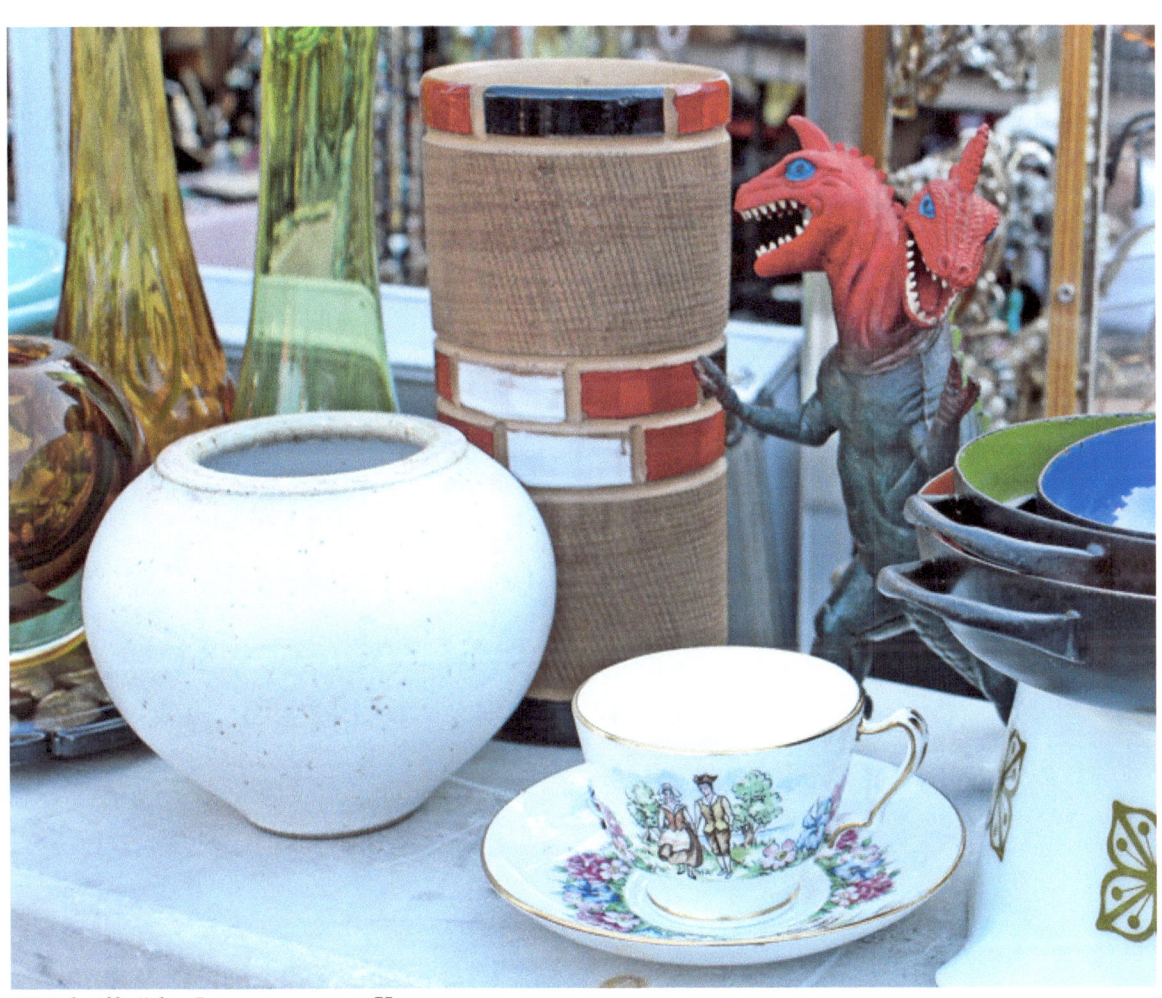
"Dishzilla" by Lawrence von Knorr

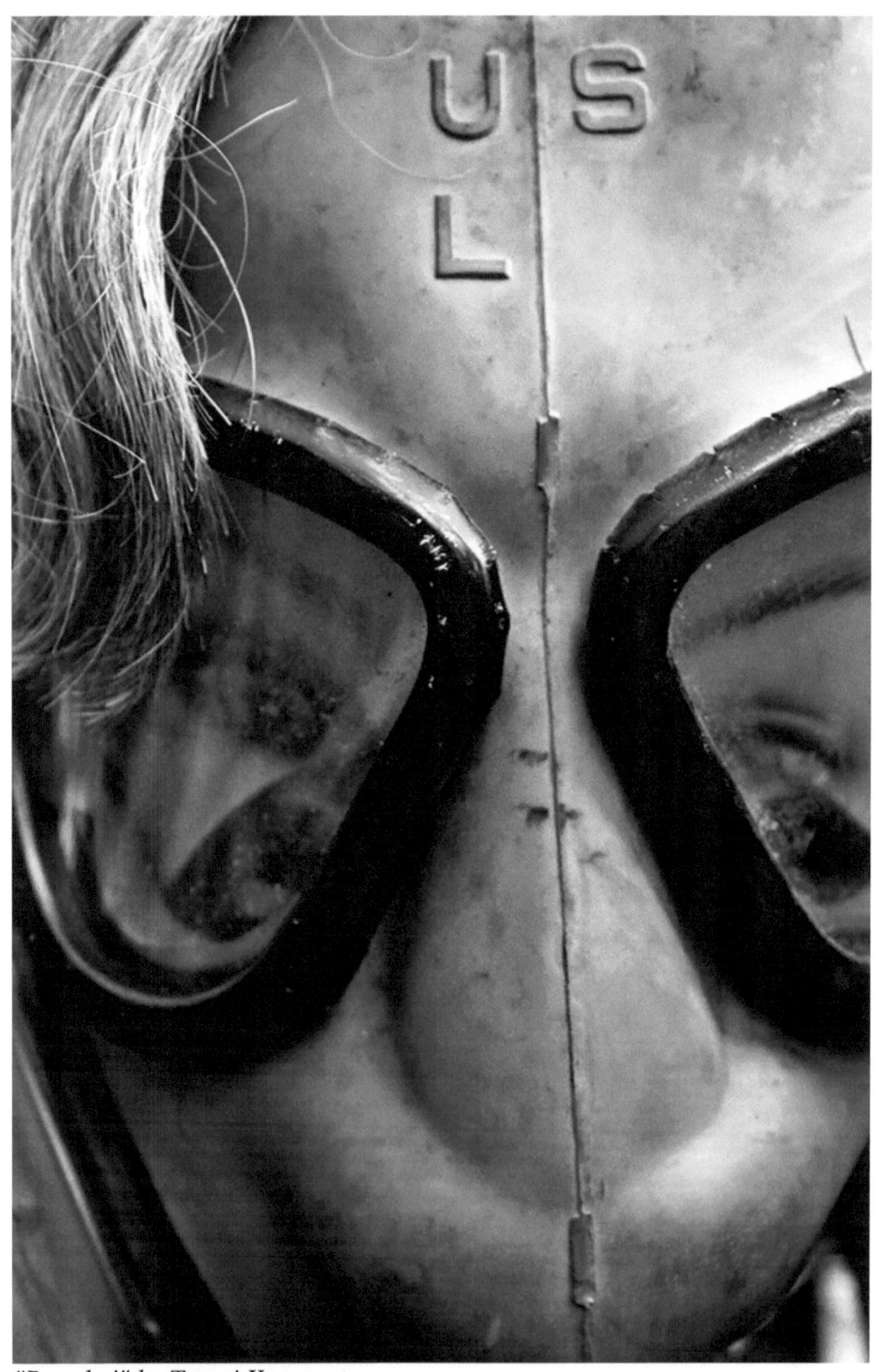
"Breathe!" by Tammi Knorr

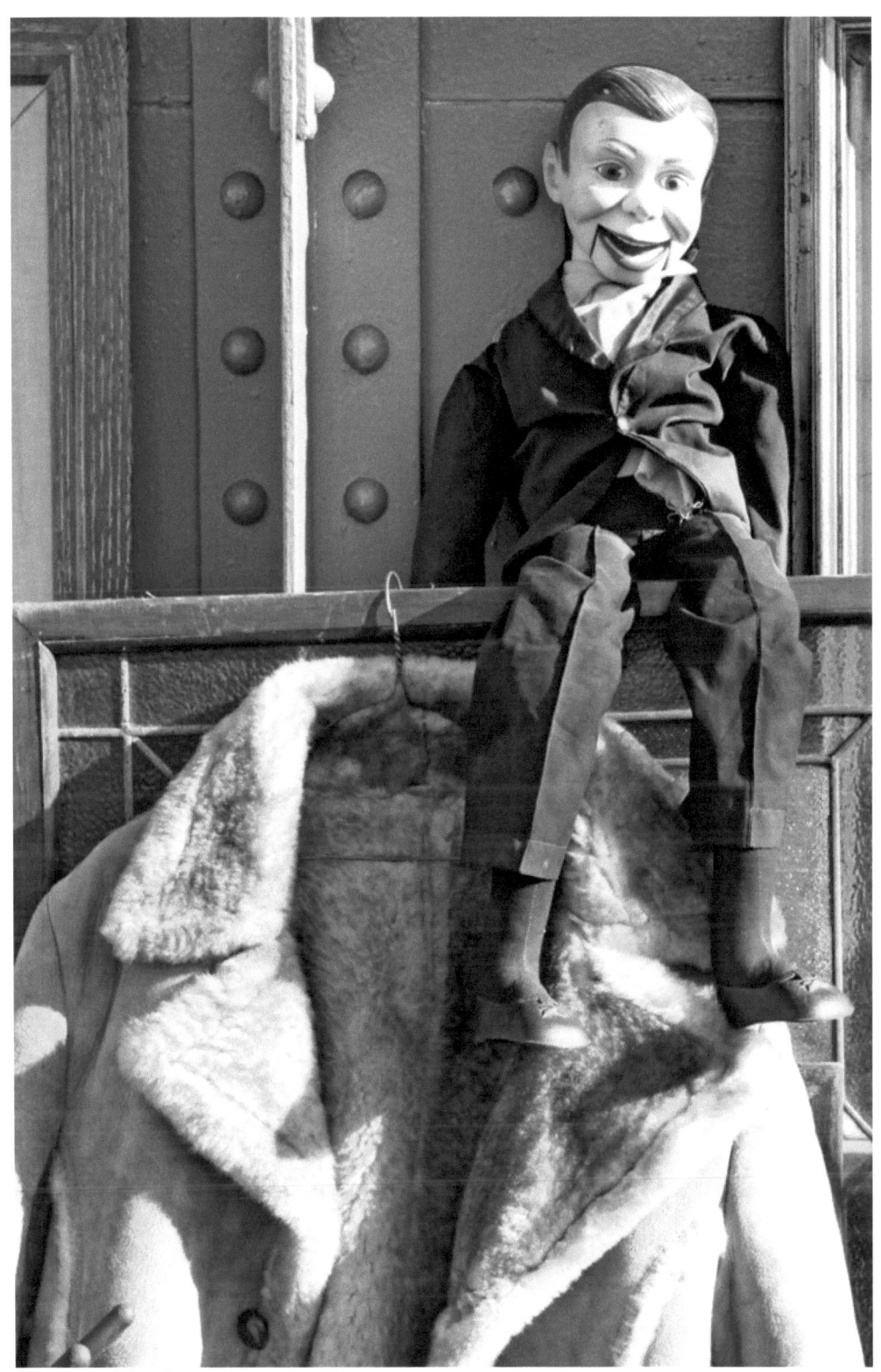

"Dummy" by Lawrence von Knorr

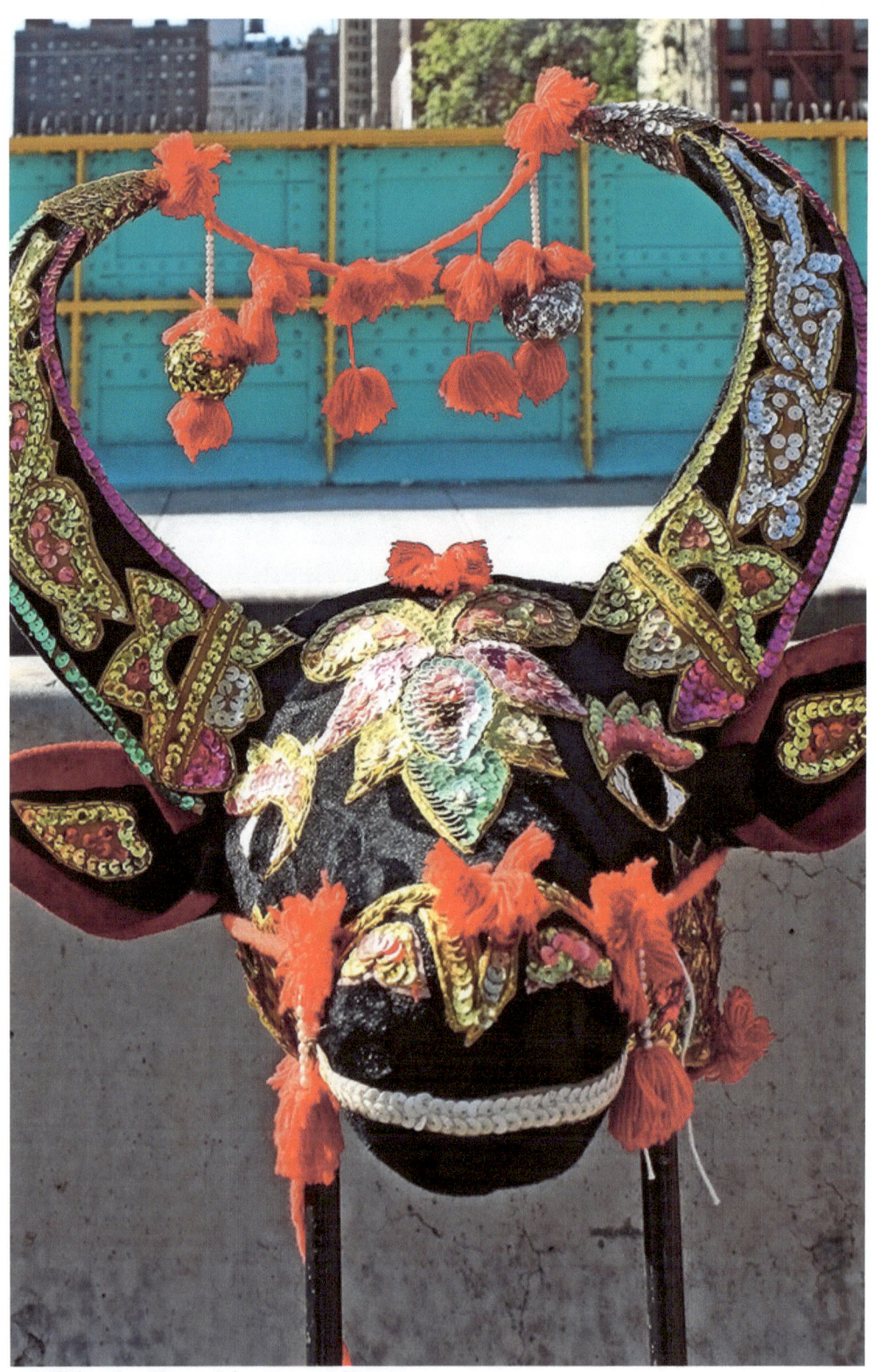

"Bull by the Horns" by Tammi Knorr

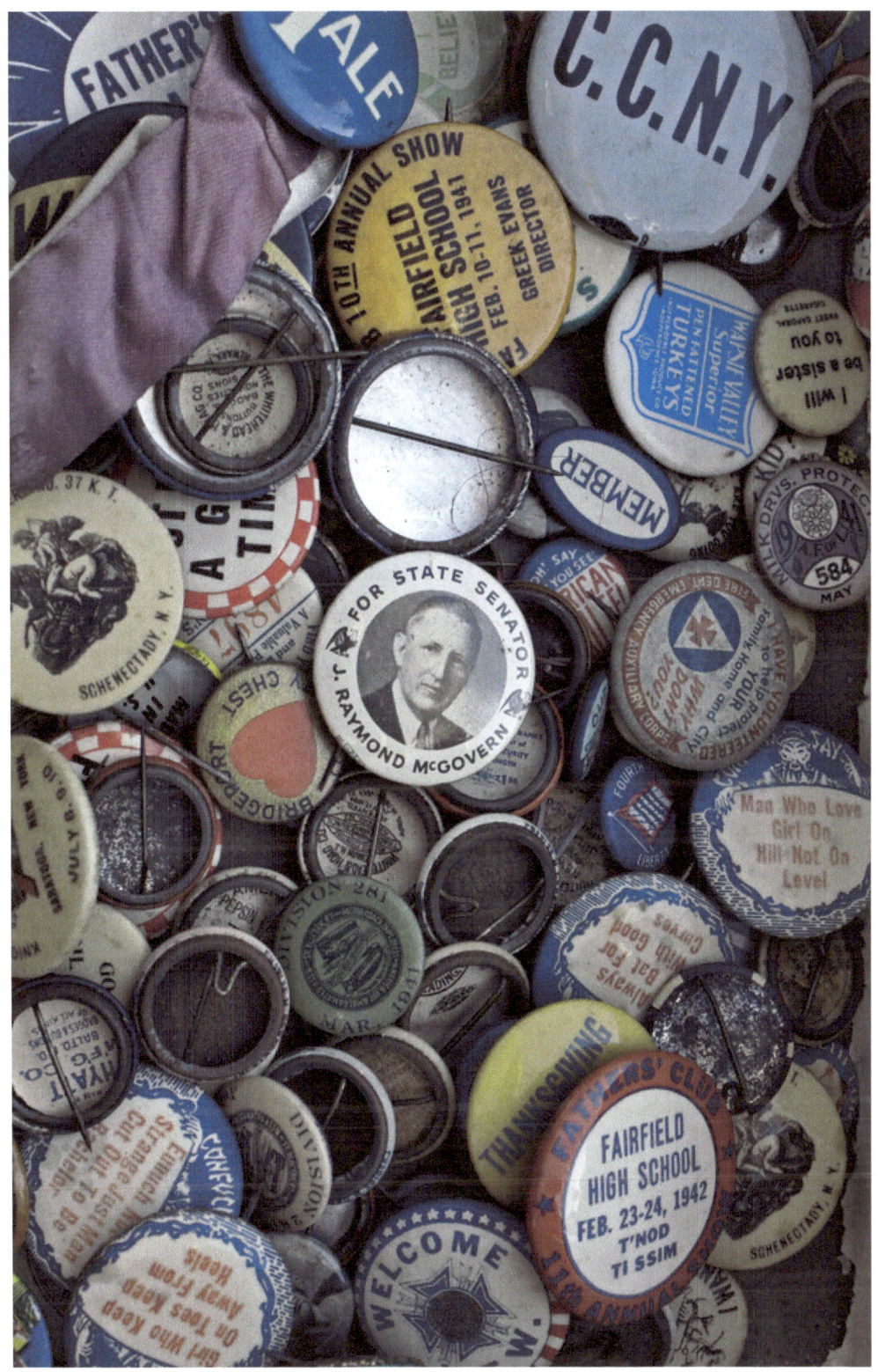
"Buttons" by Tammi Knorr

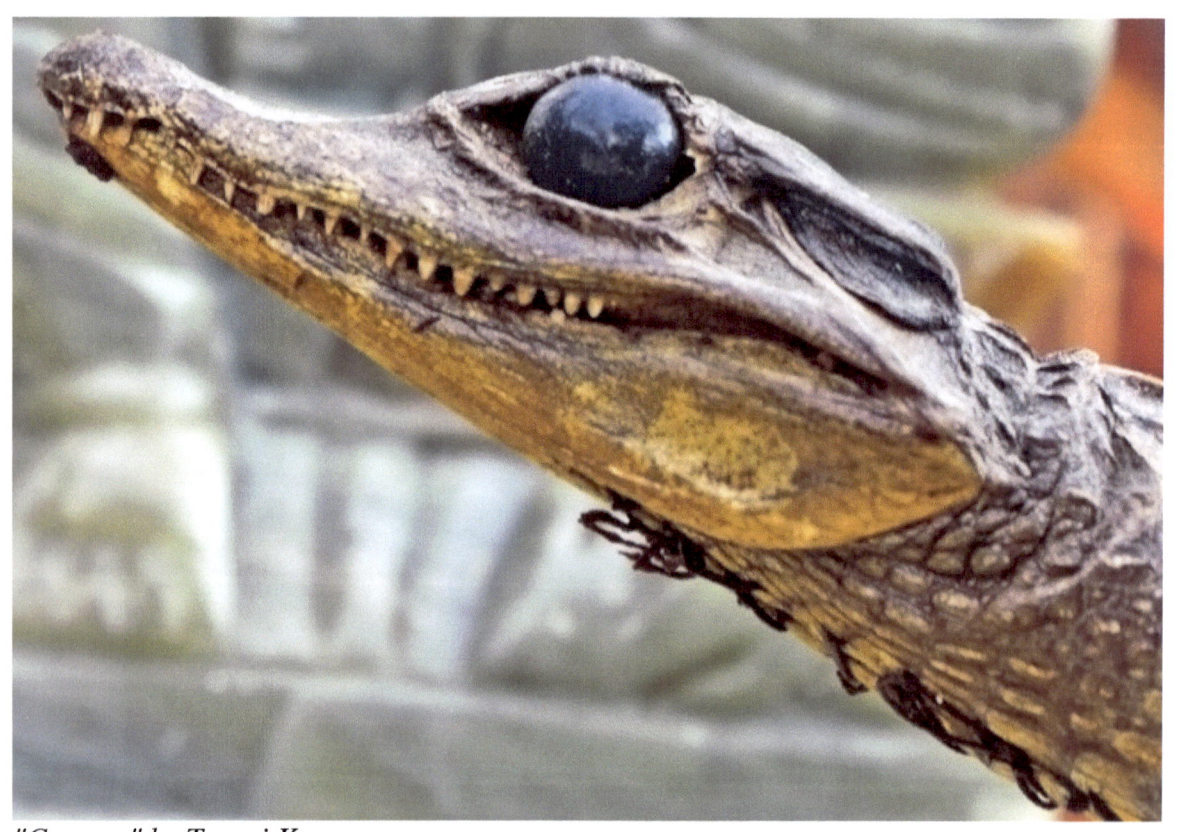

"Cayman" by Tammi Knorr

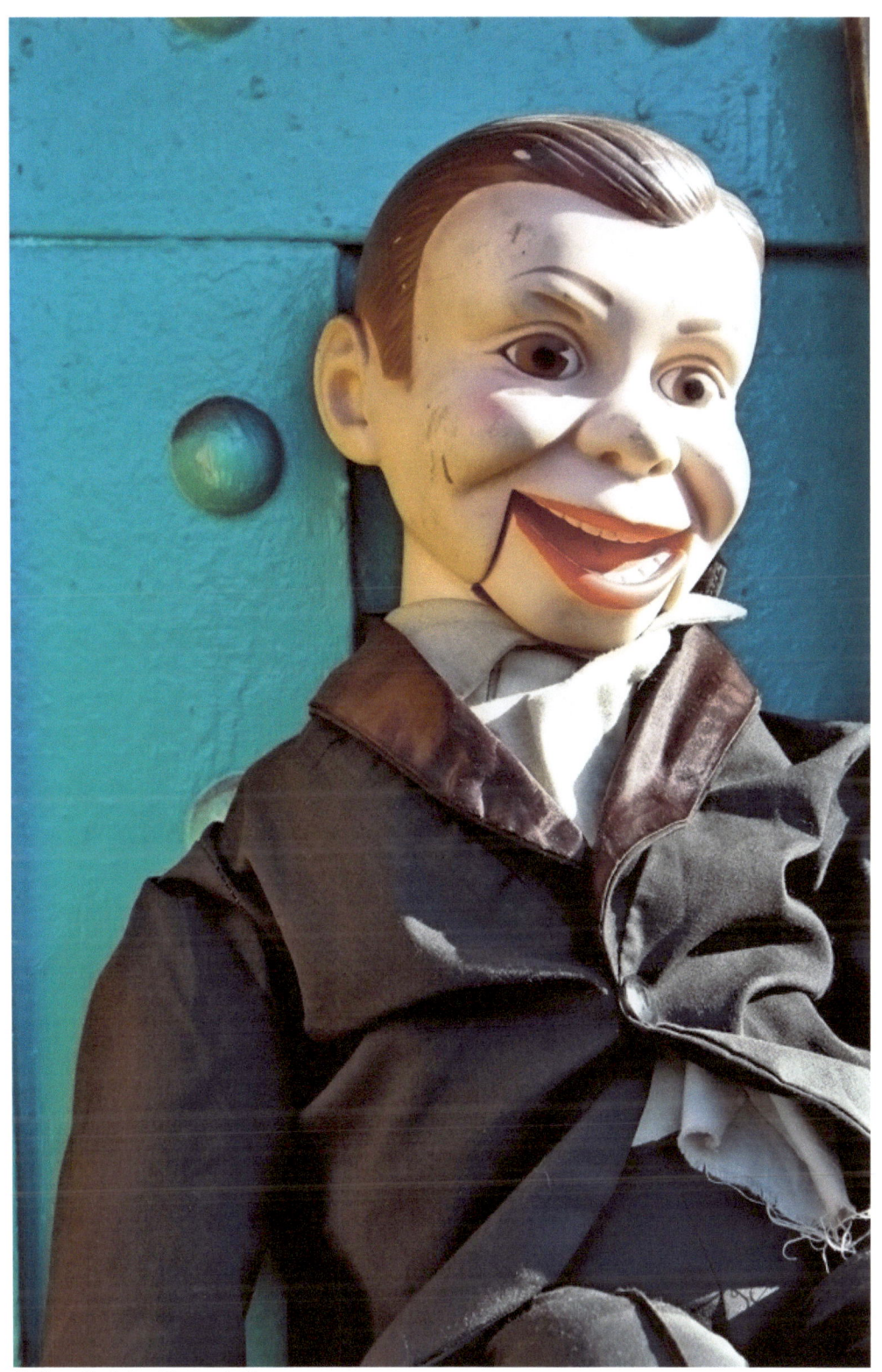

"Charlie" by Tammi Knorr

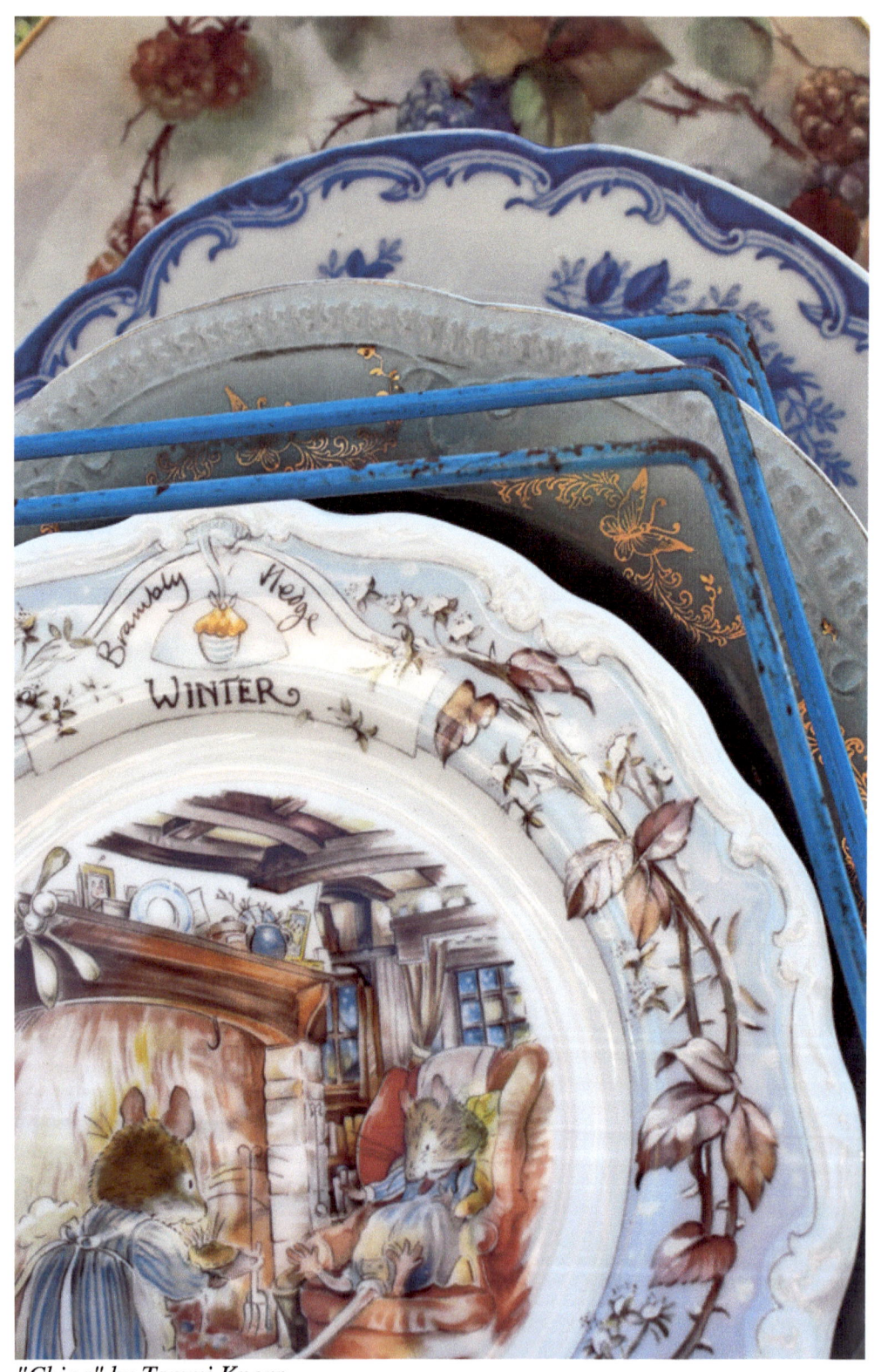

"China" by Tammi Knorr

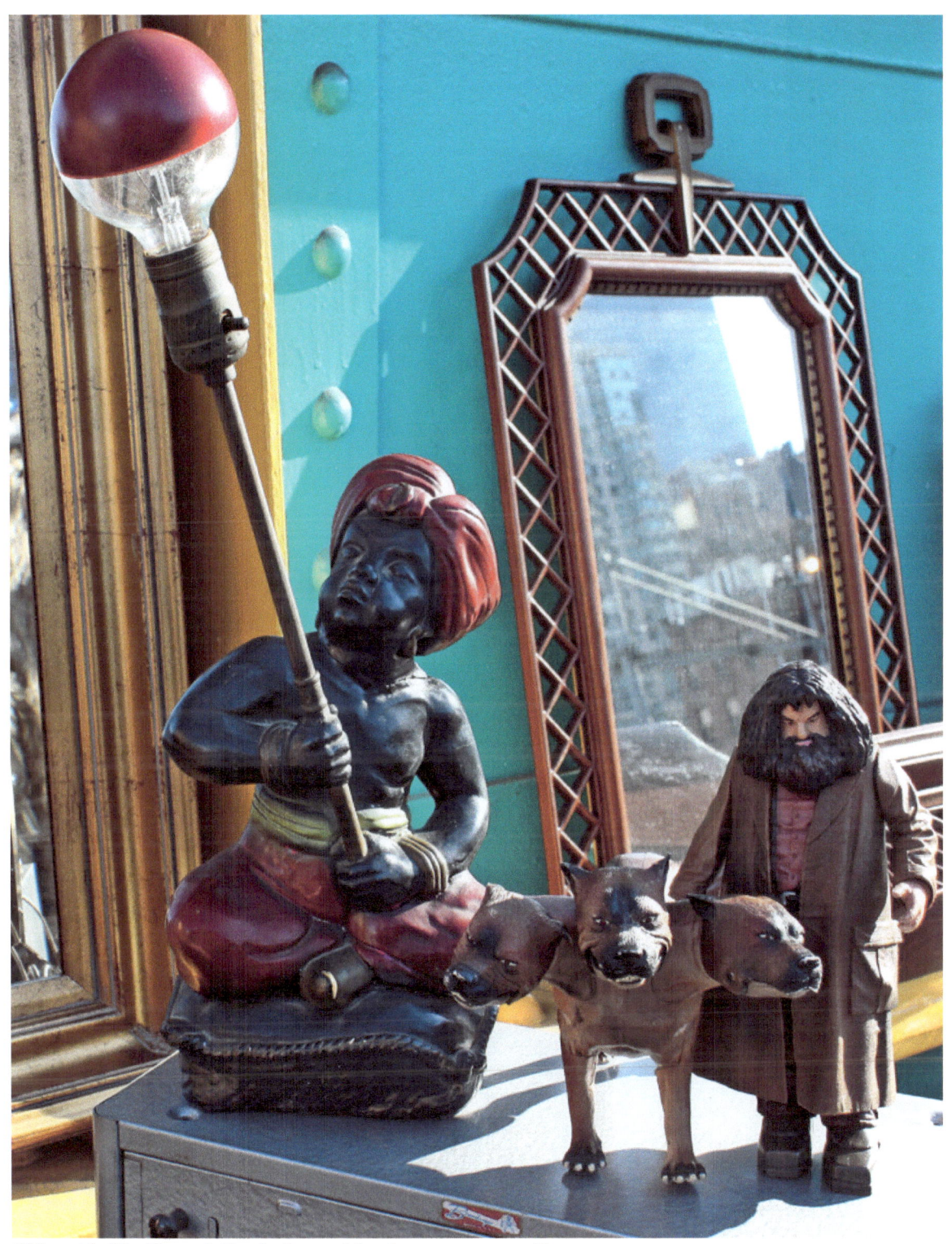
"Hagrid, Fluffy and Genie Lamp" by Lawrence von Knorr

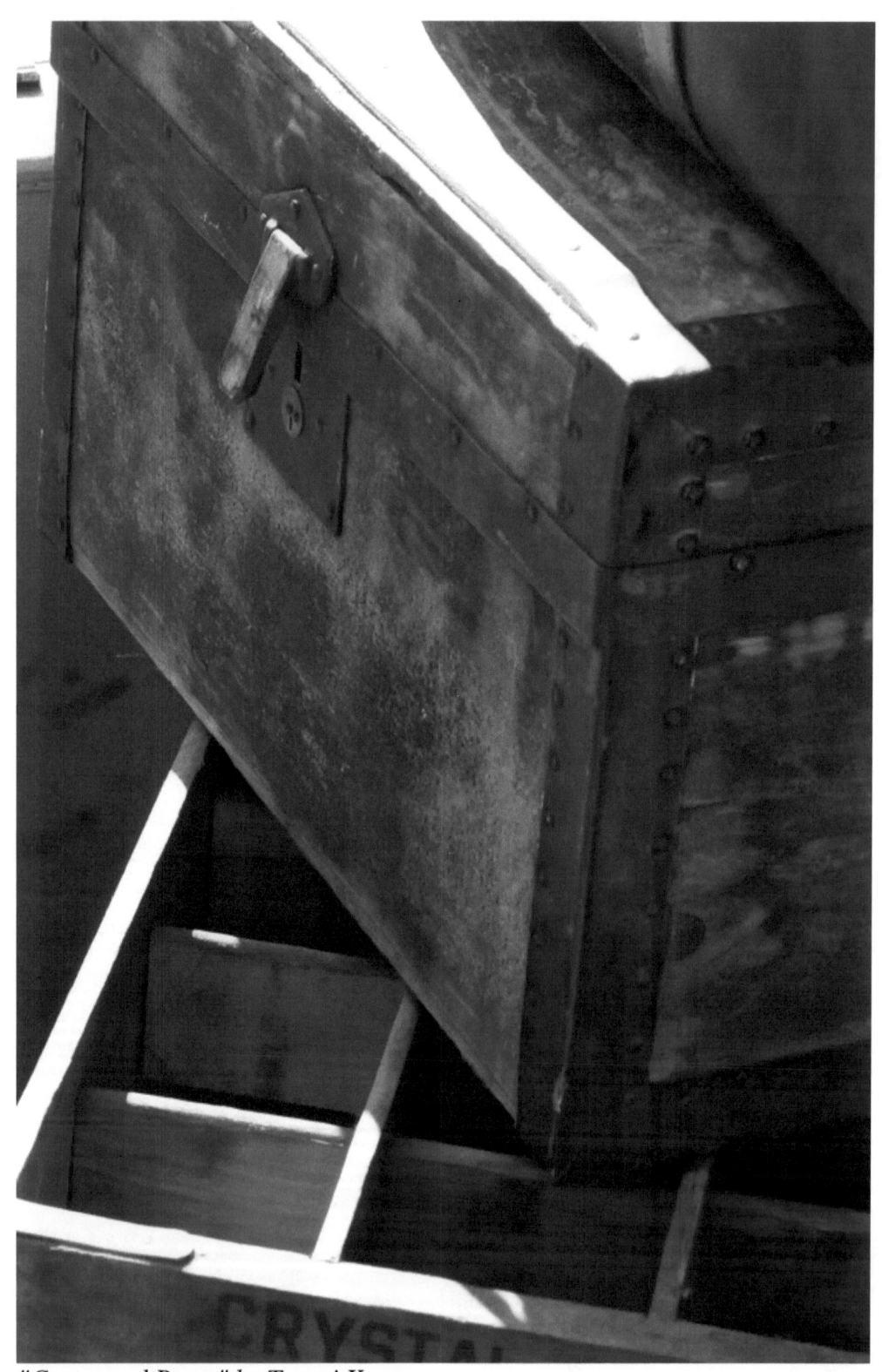
"Crates and Boxes" by Tammi Knorr

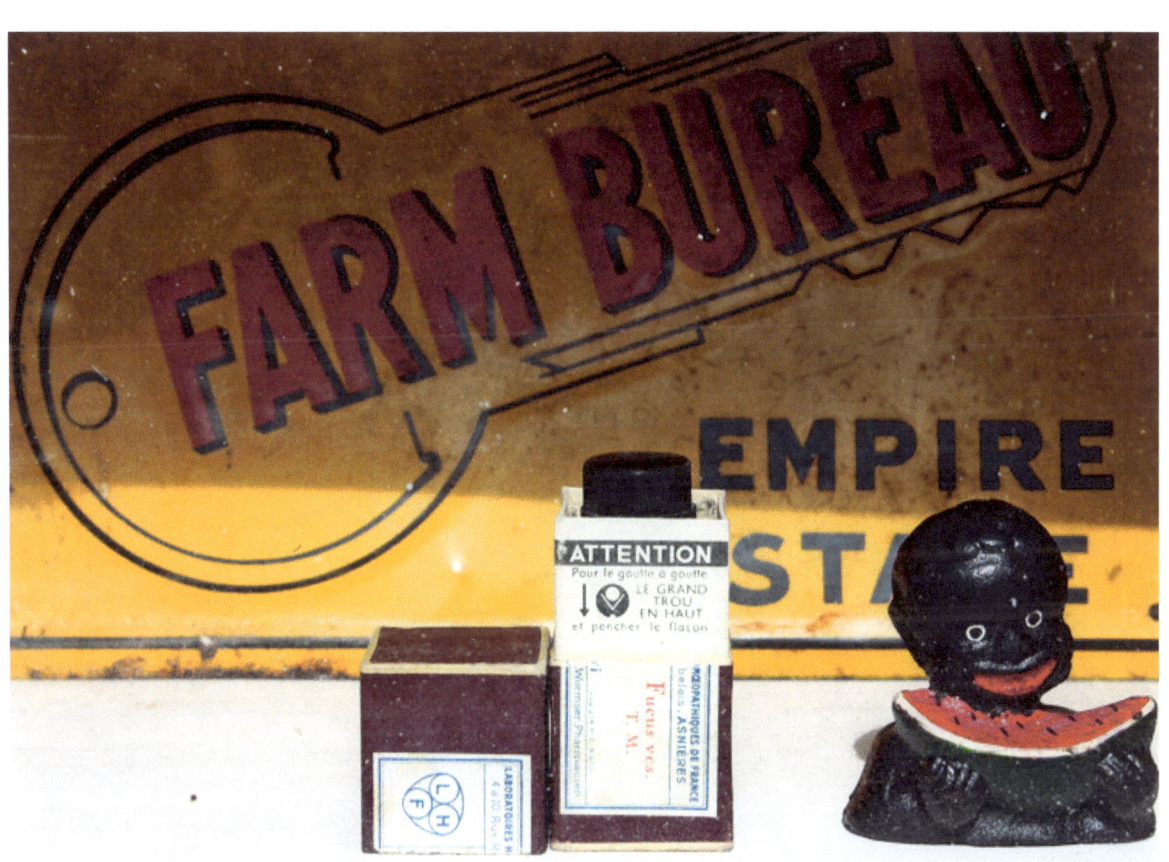

"Farm Empire" by Tammi Knorr

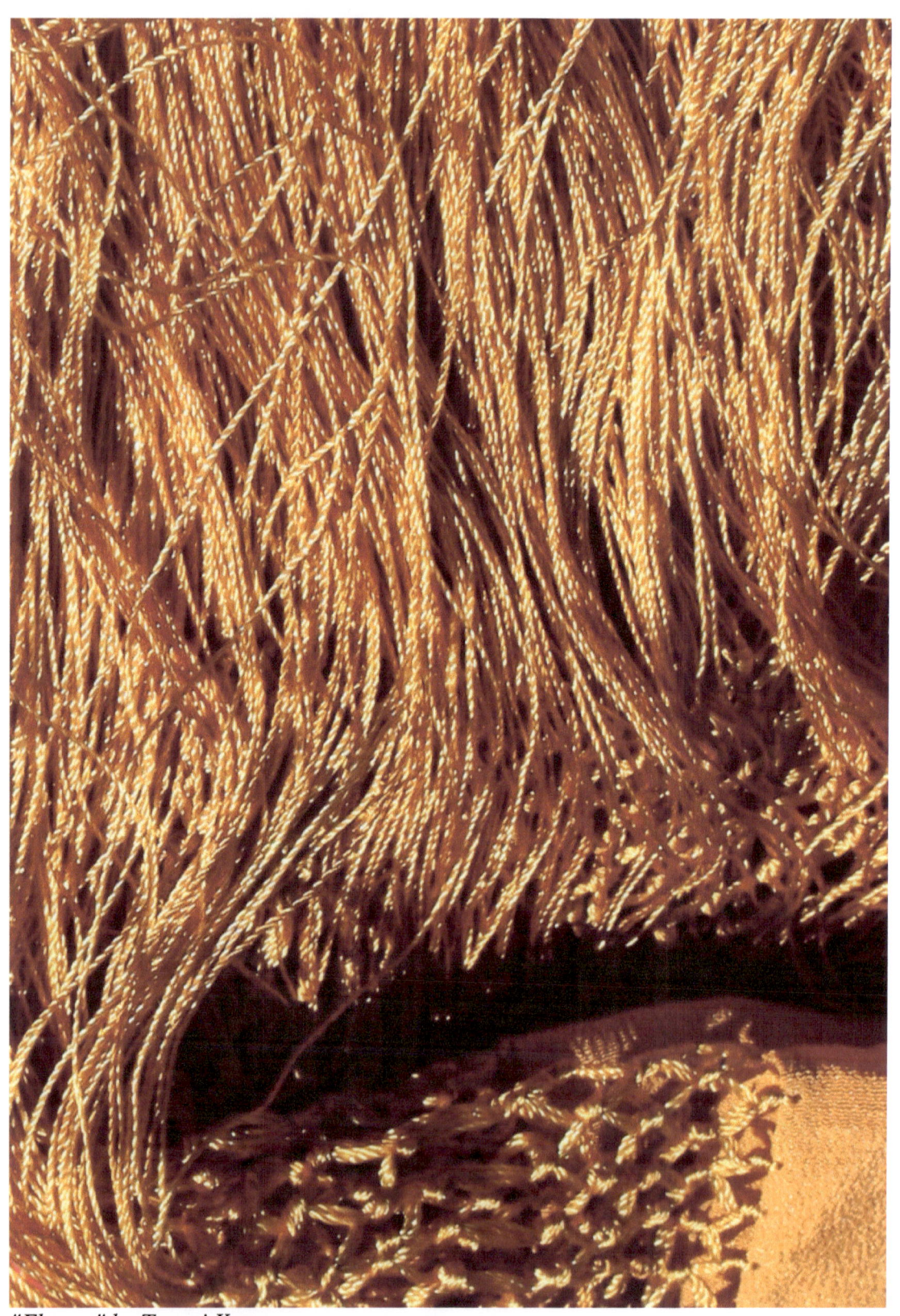
"Flames" by Tammi Knorr

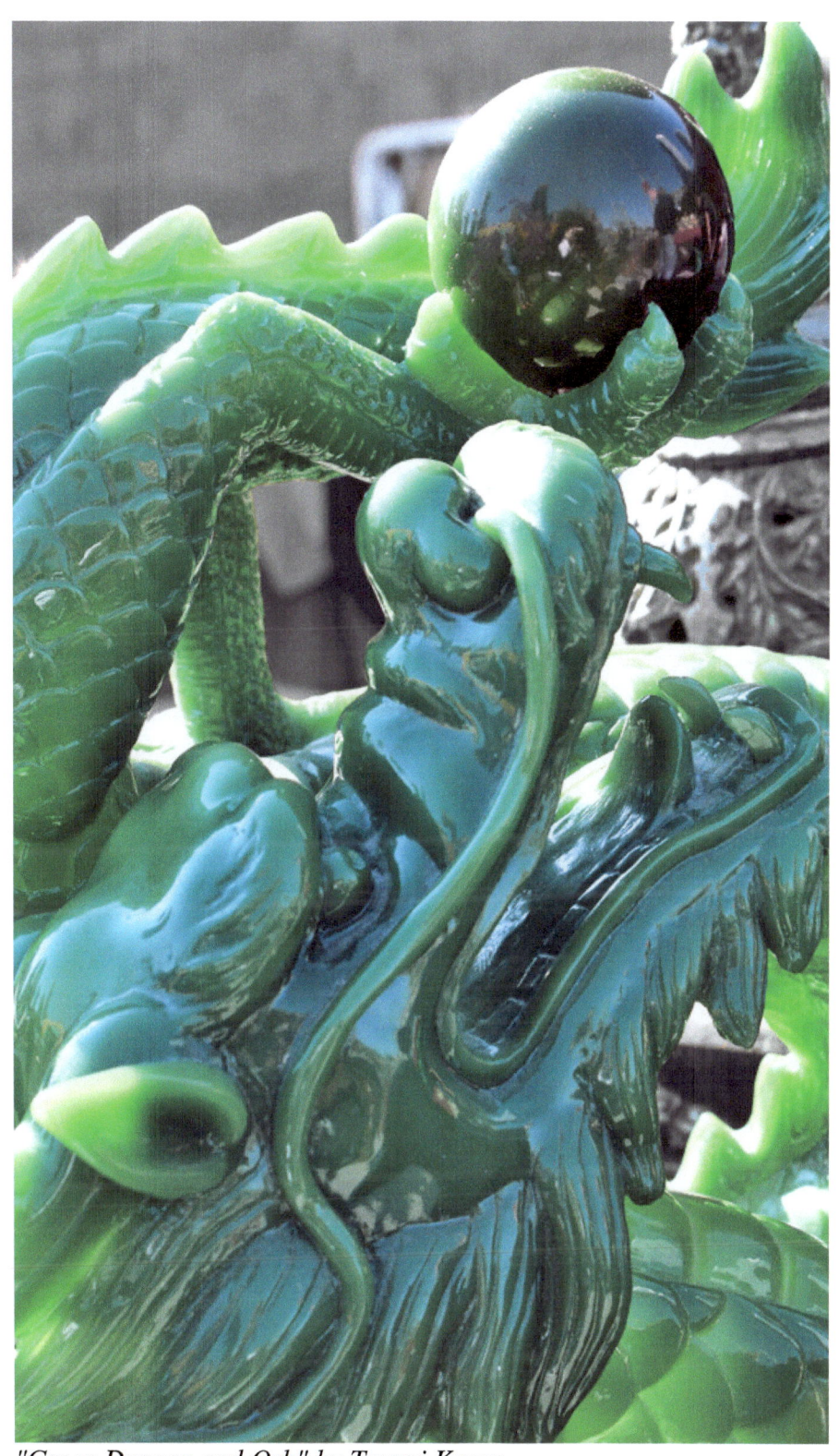

"Green Dragon and Orb" by Tammi Knorr

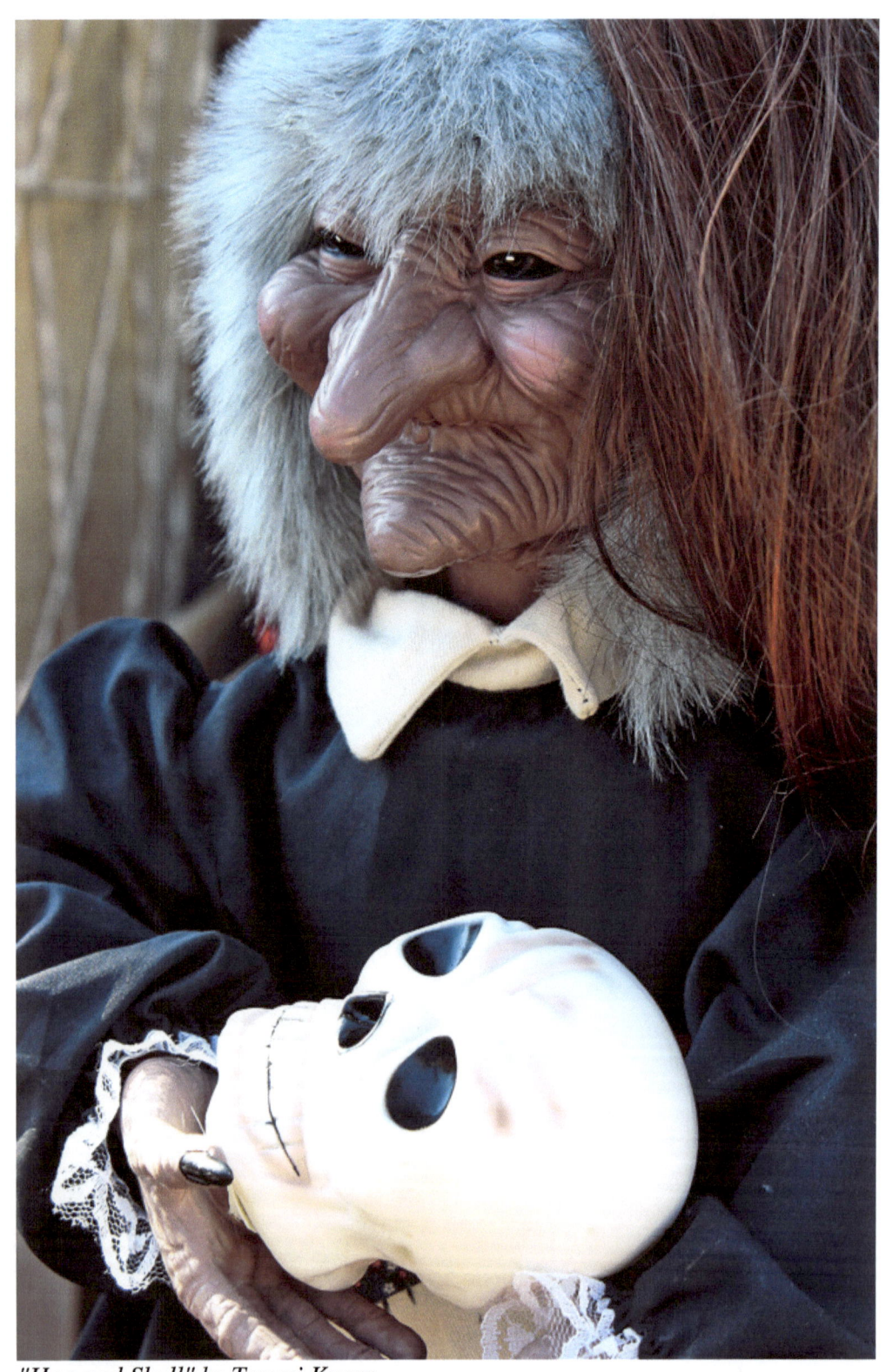

"Hag and Skull" by Tammi Knorr

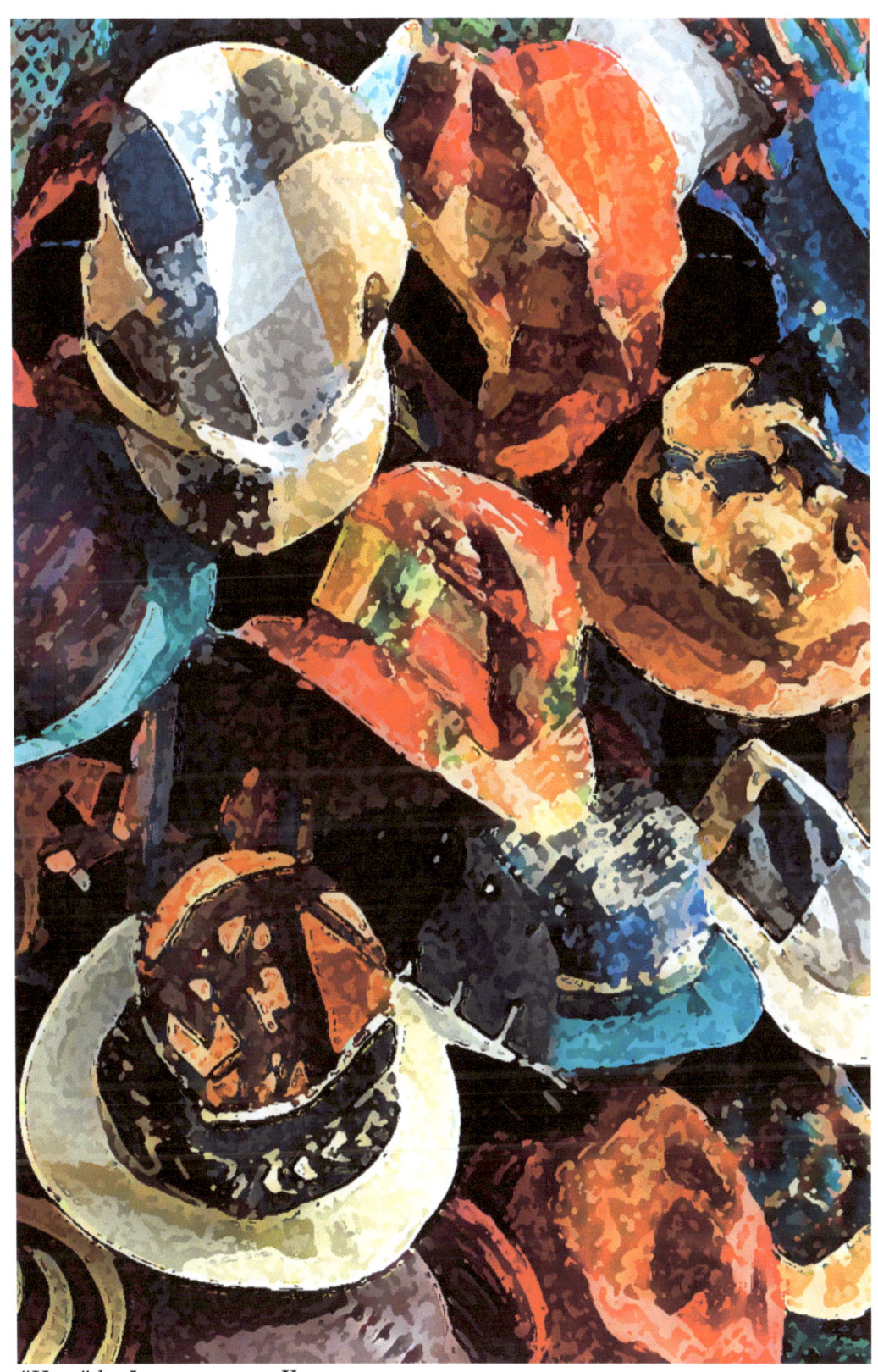

"Hats" by Lawrence von Knorr

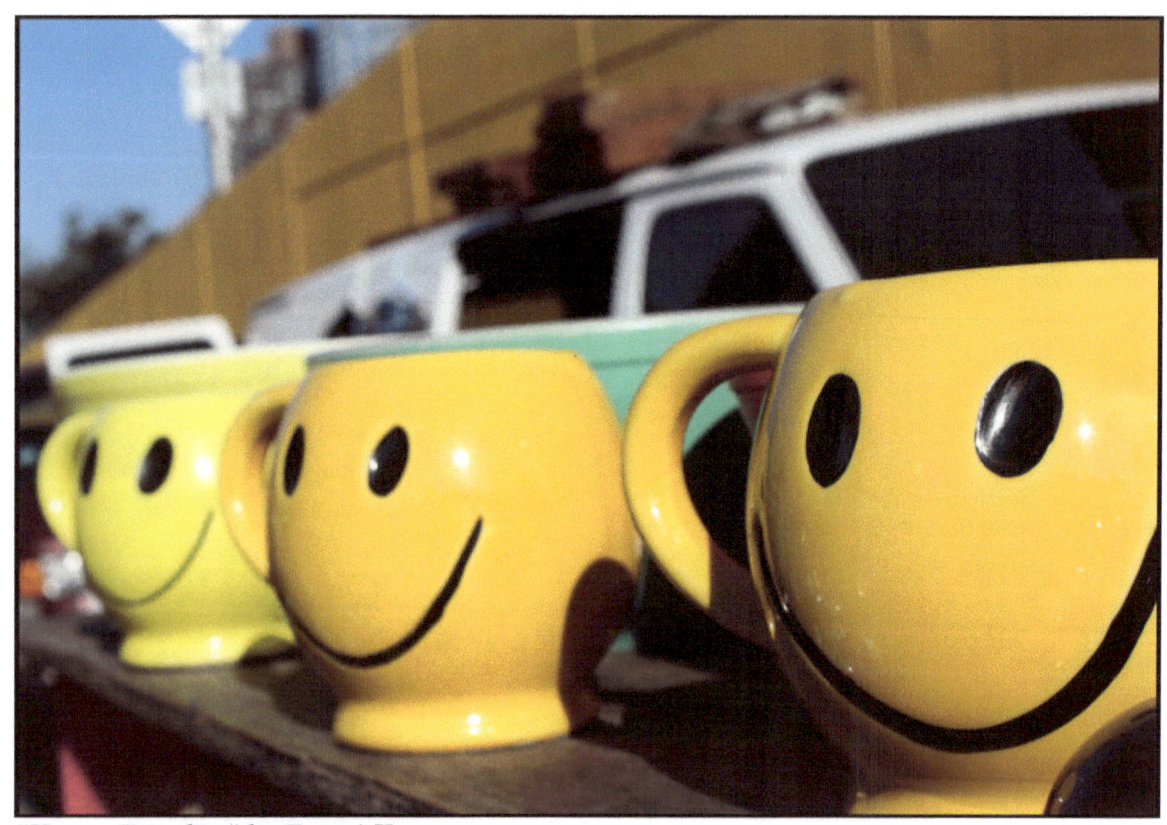
"Happy Together" by Tammi Knorr

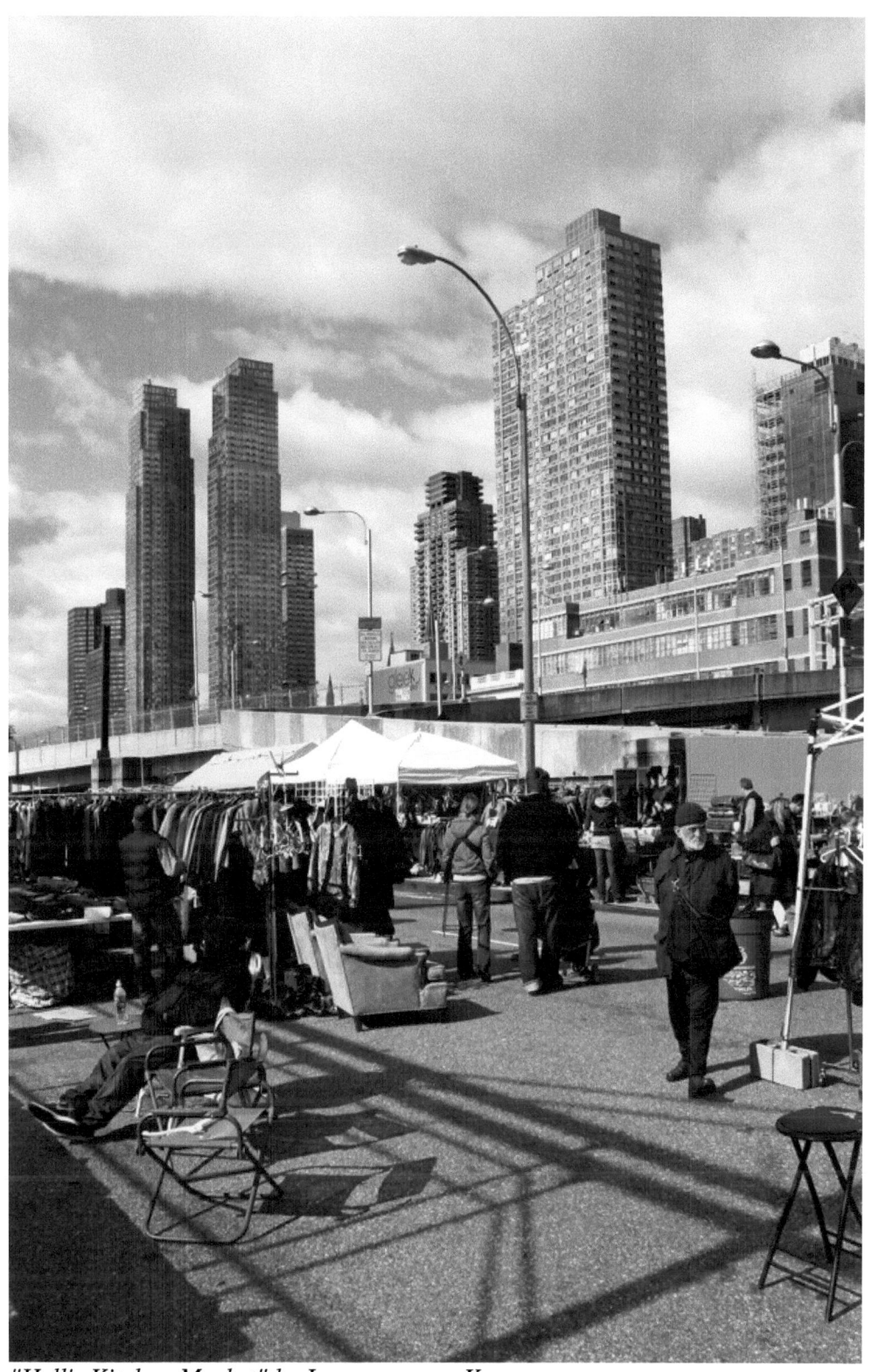

"Hell's Kitchen Market" by Lawrence von Knorr

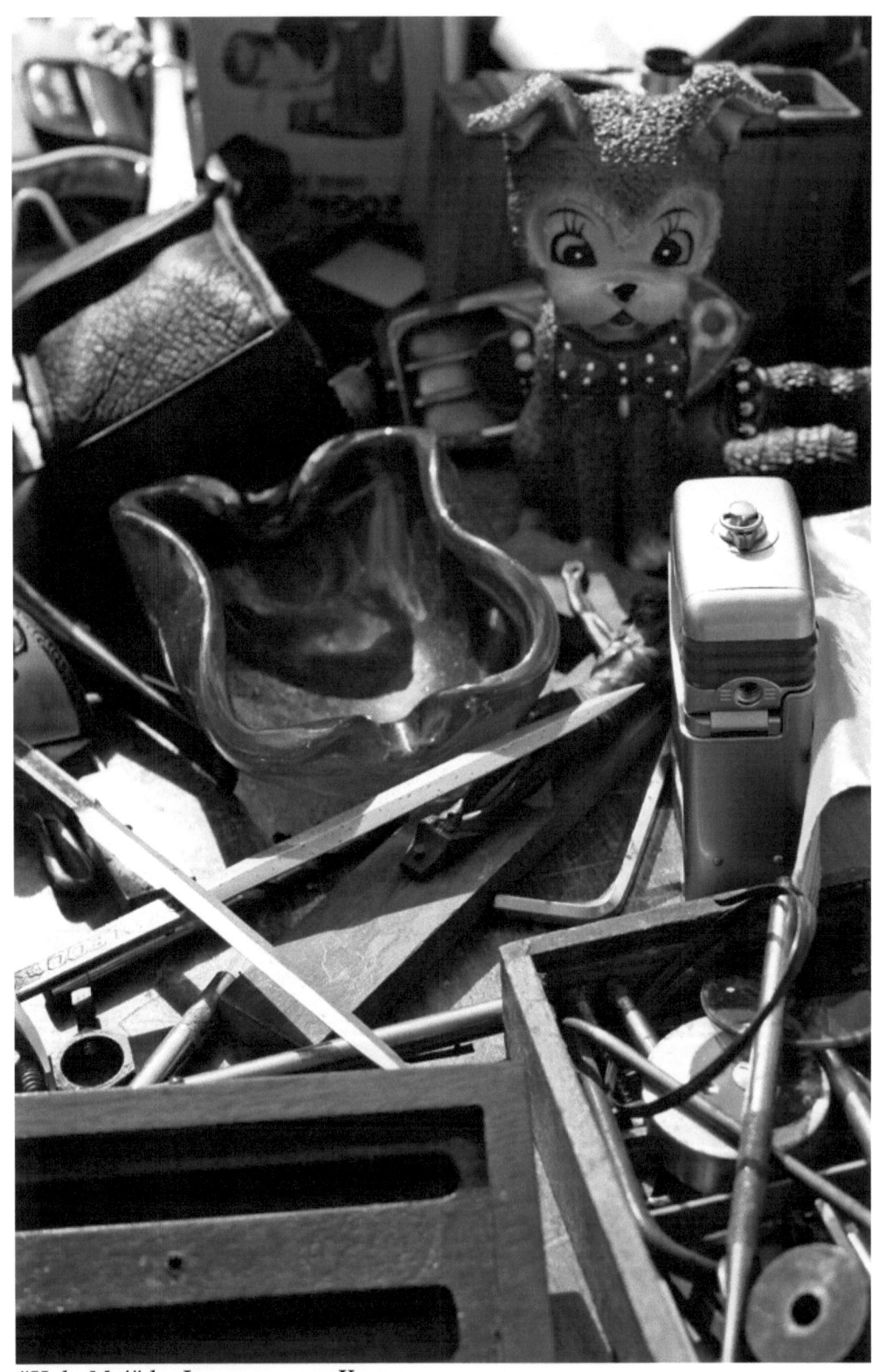

"Help Me!" by Lawrence von Knorr

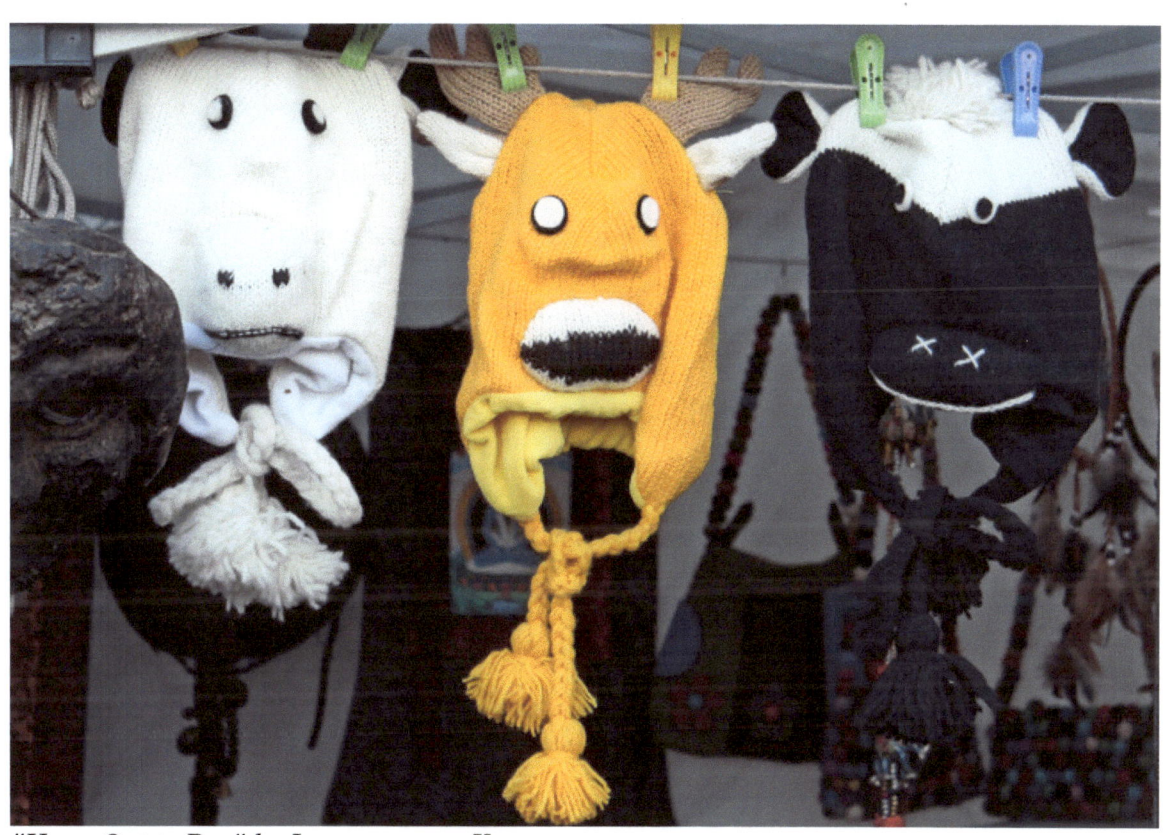
"Hung Out to Dry" by Lawrence von Knorr

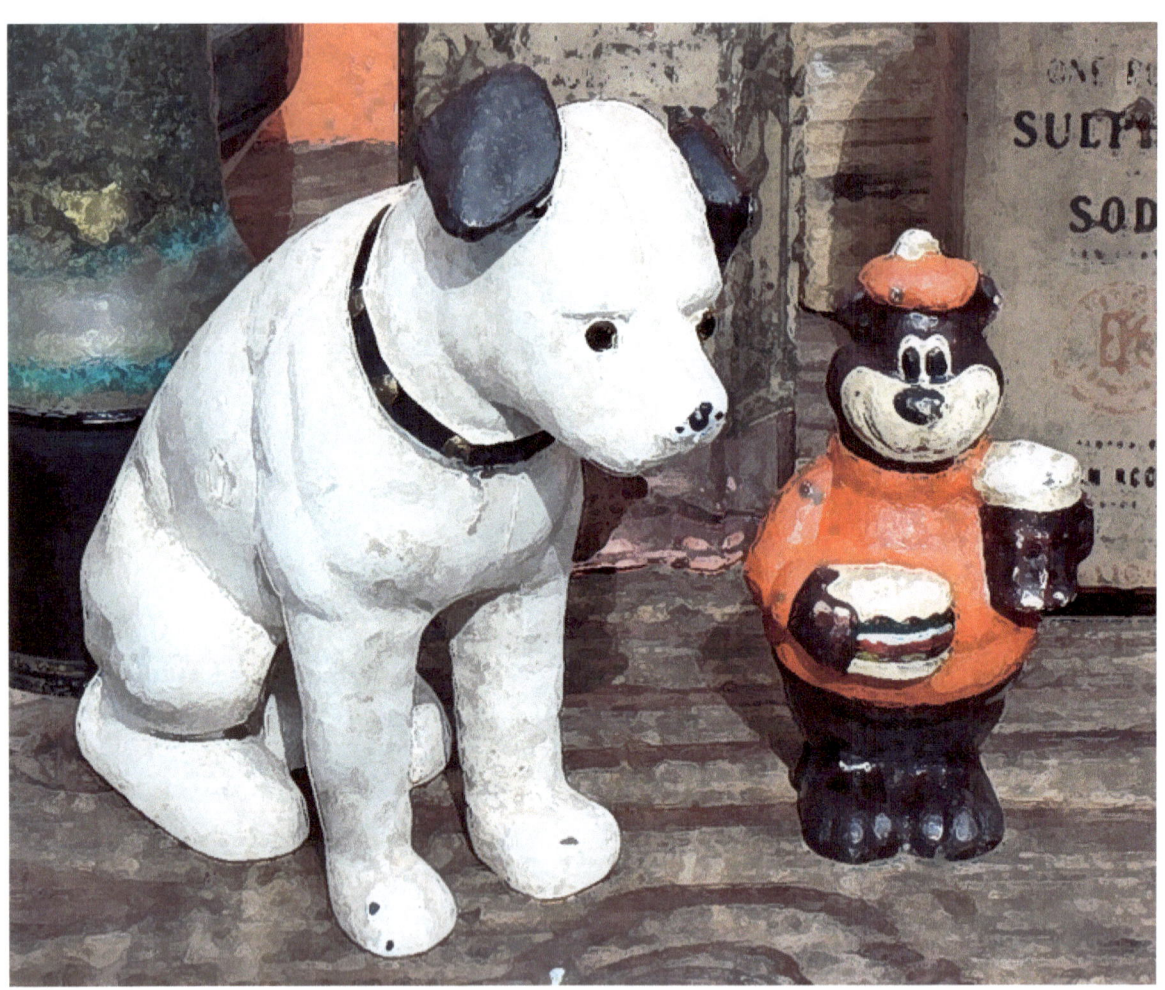
"Hungry Dog" by Lawrence von Knorr

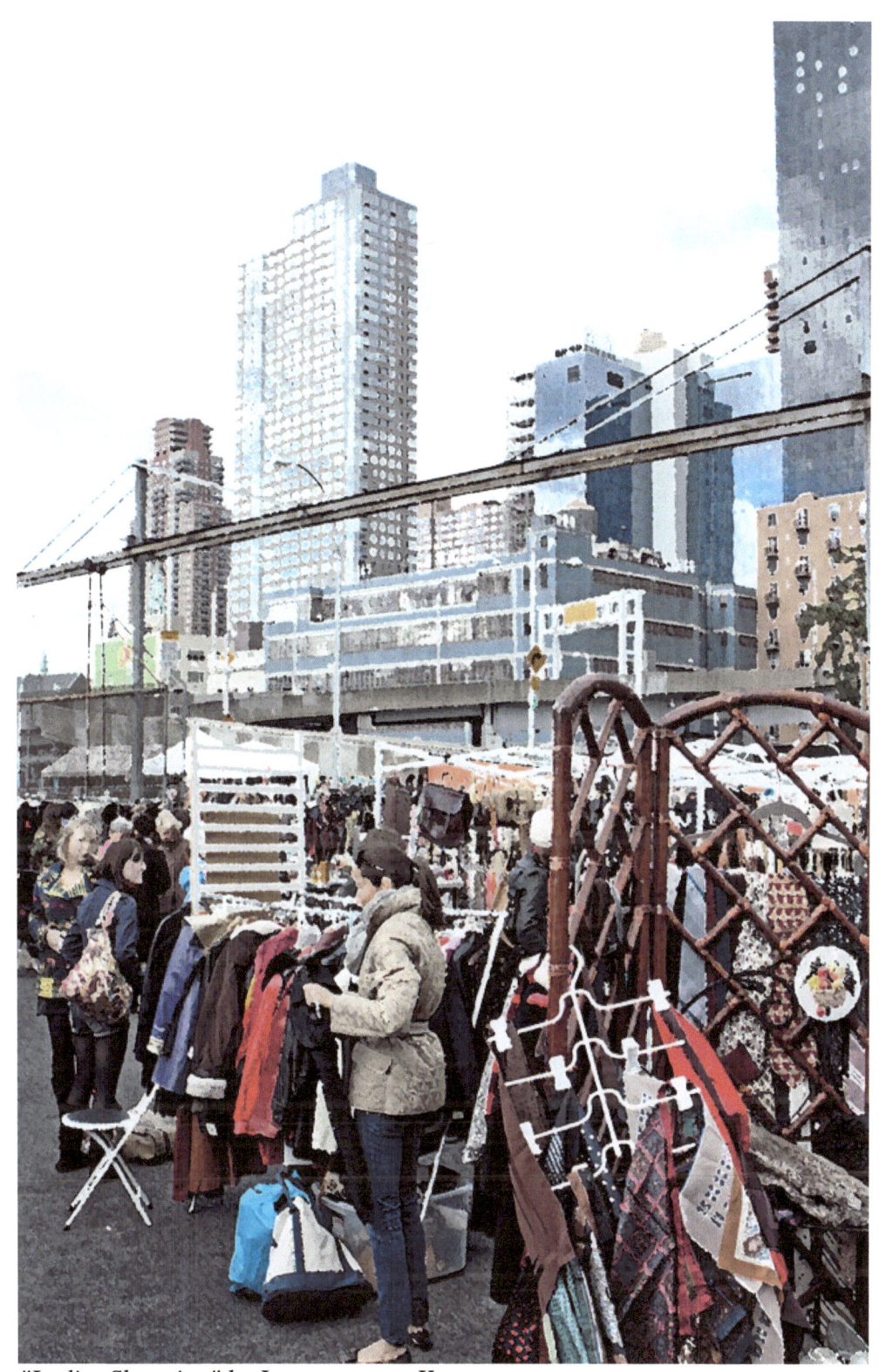

"Ladies Shopping" by Lawrence von Knorr

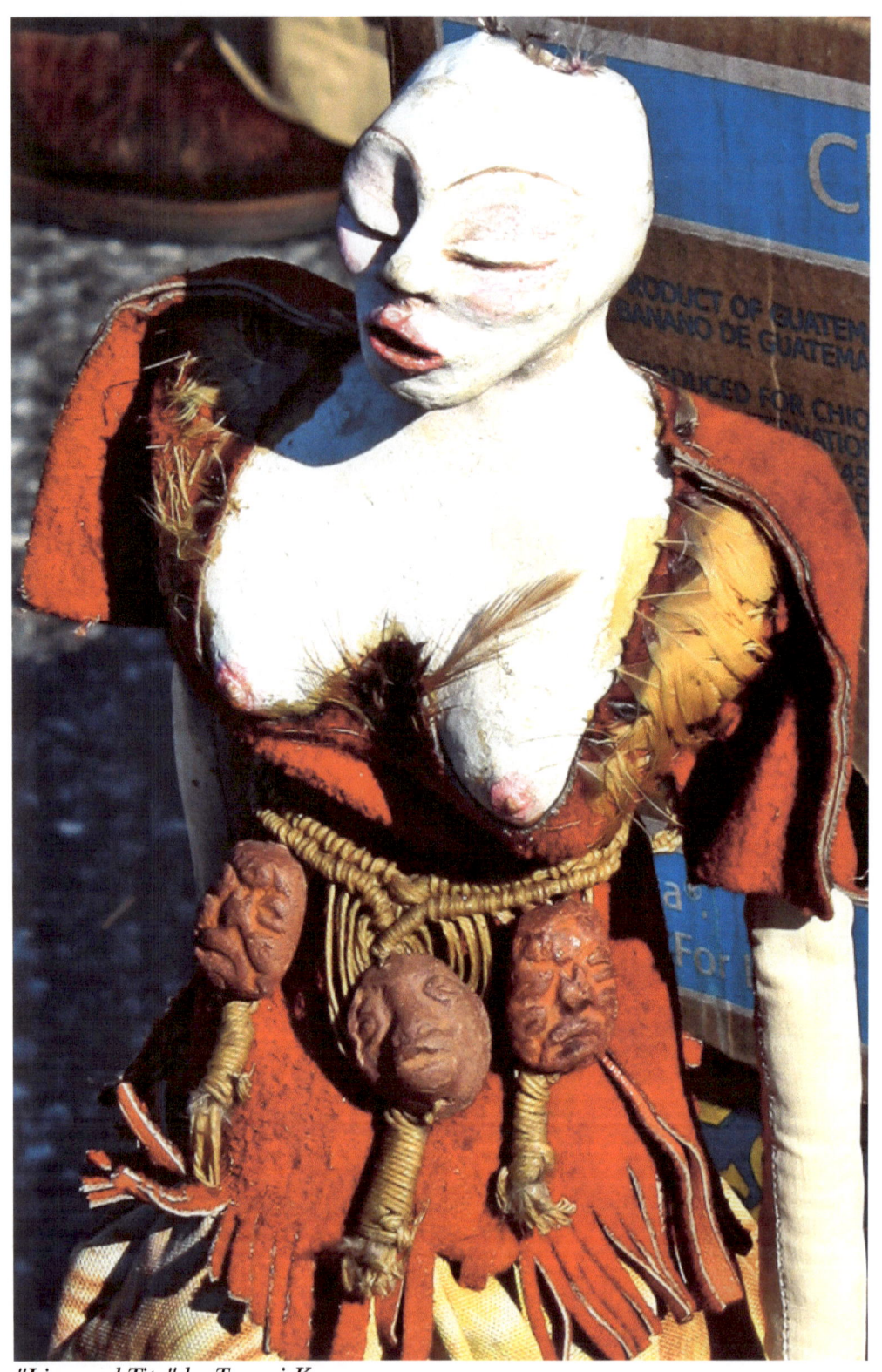

"Lips and Tits" by Tammi Knorr

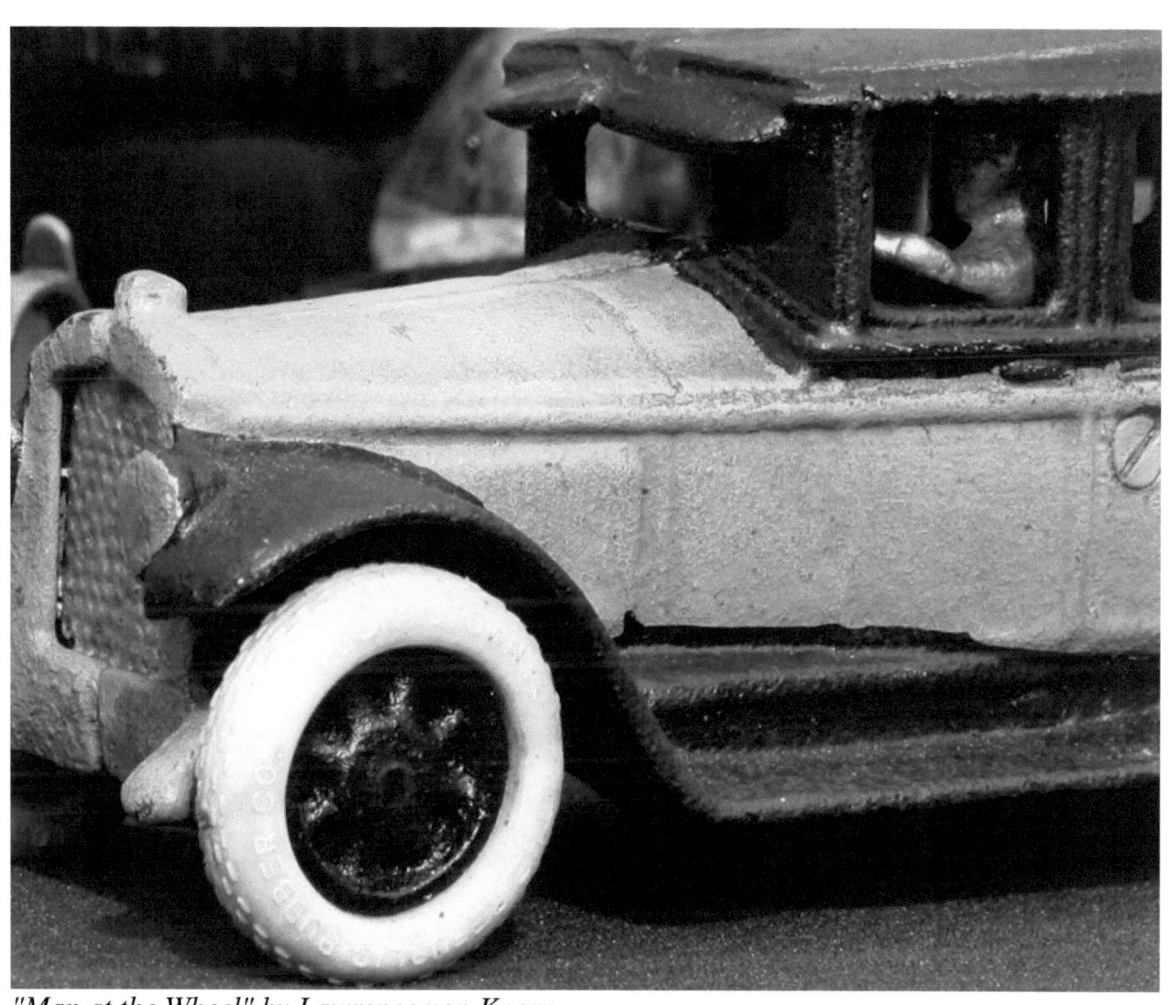
"Man at the Wheel" by Lawrence von Knorr

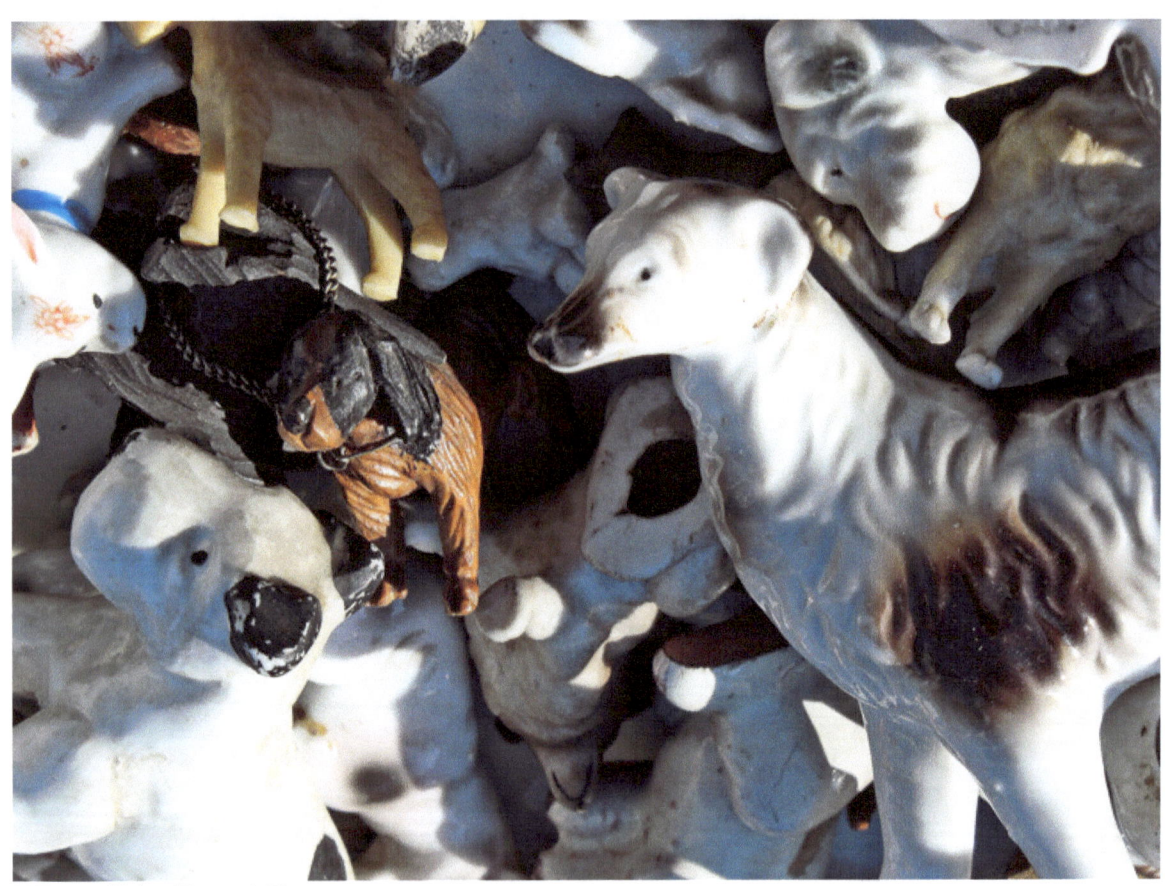

"Kennel" by Tammi Knorr

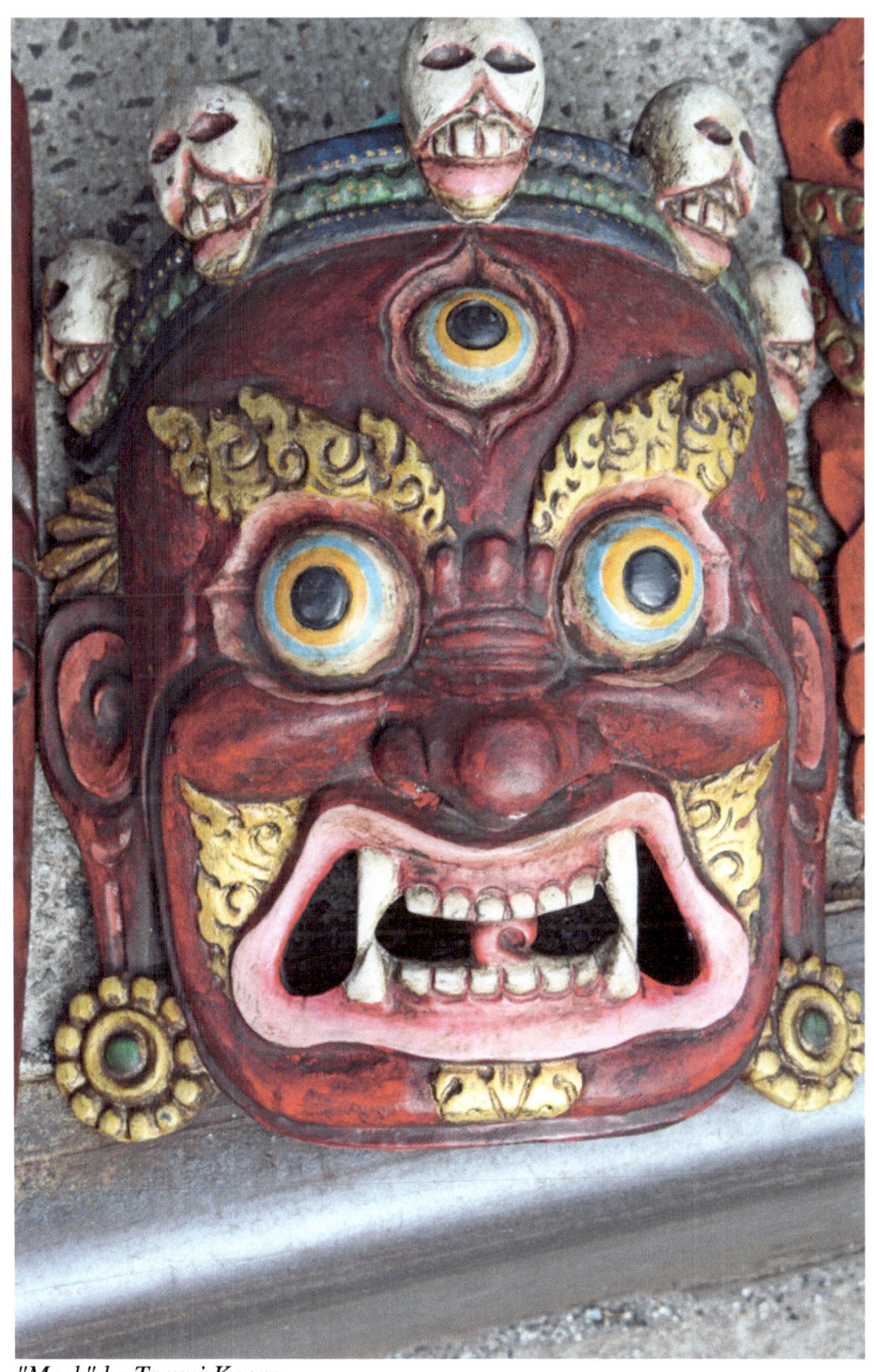
"Mask" by Tammi Knorr

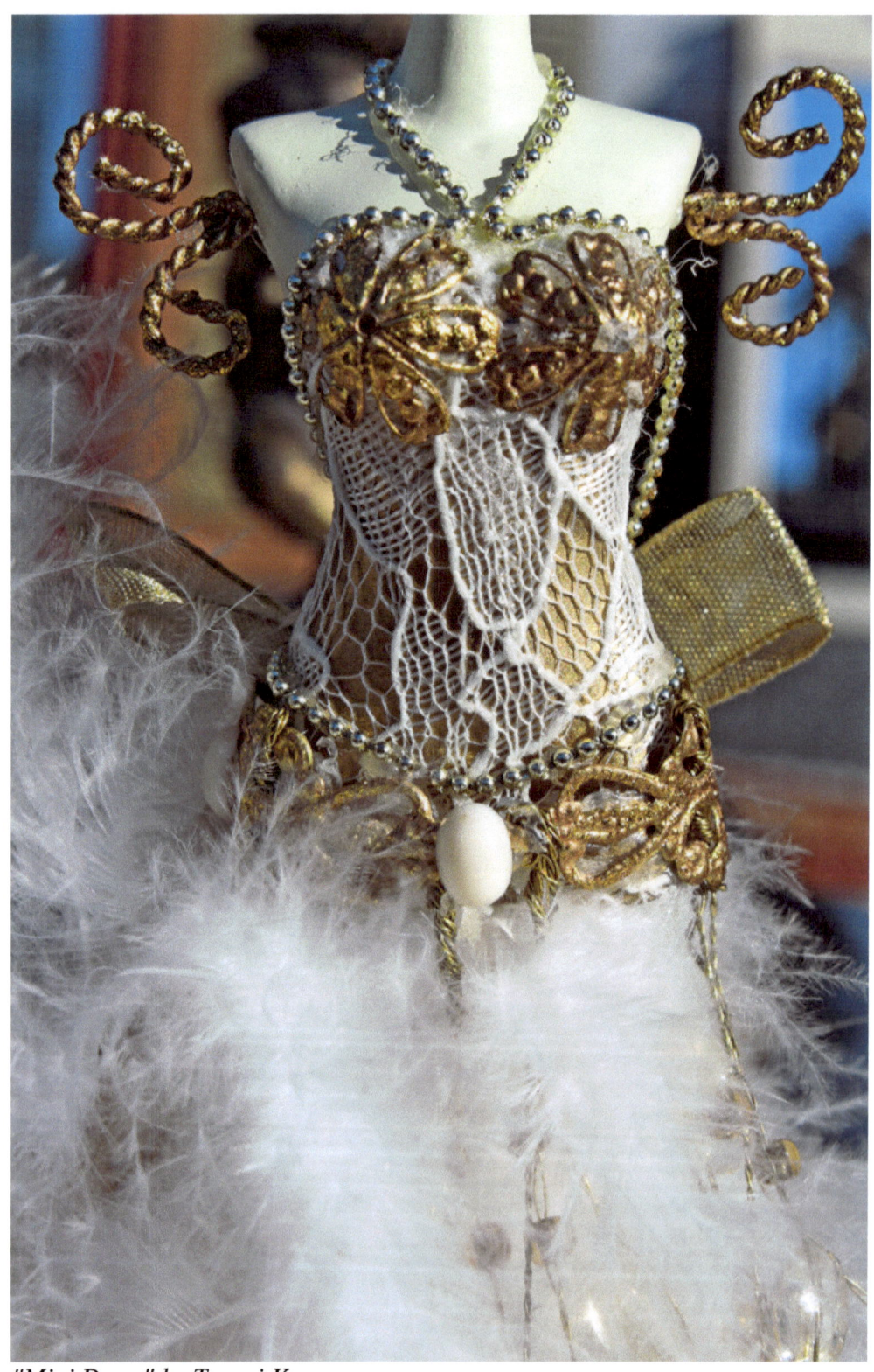

"Mini Dress" by Tammi Knorr

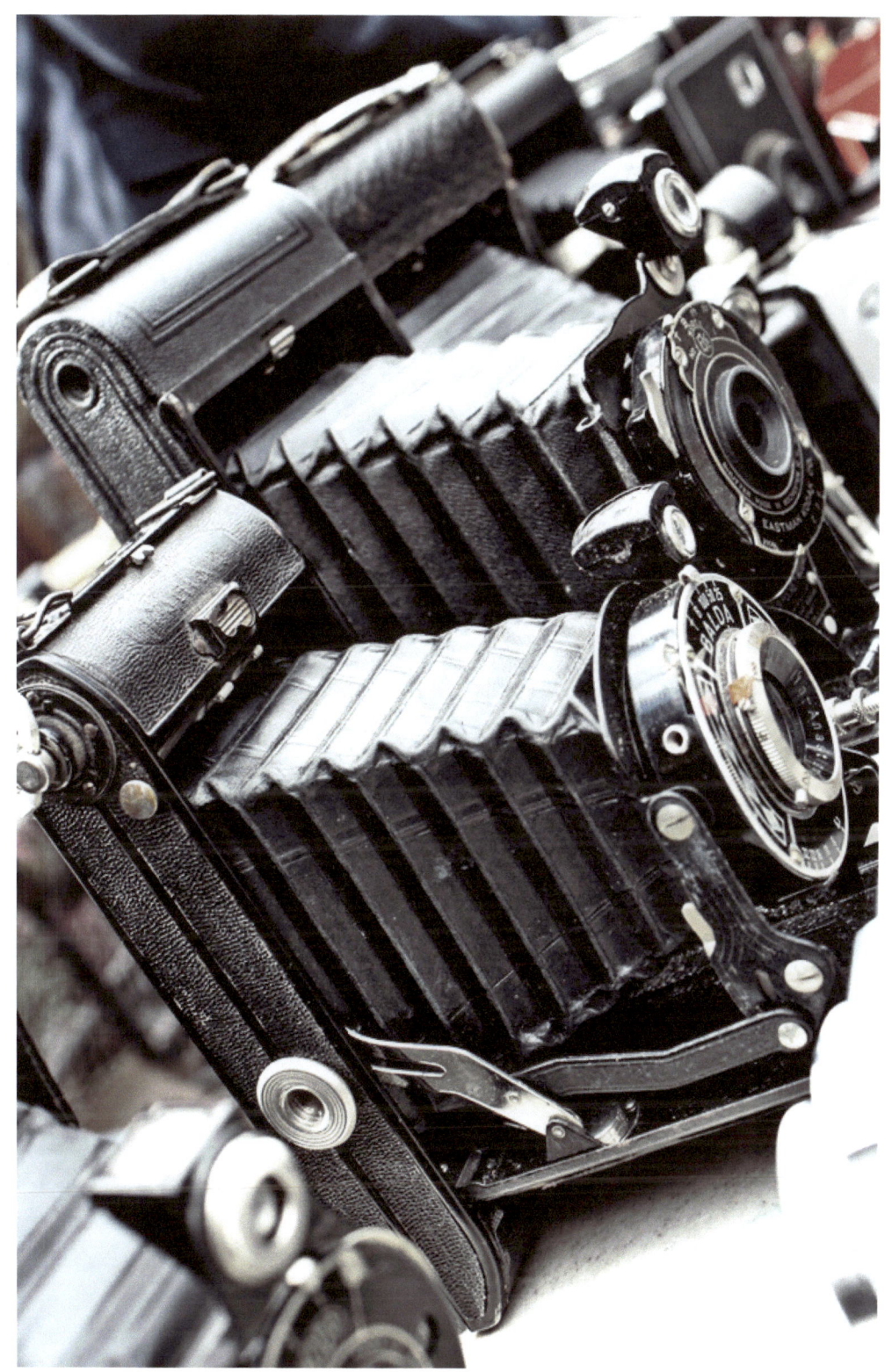
"Old Cameras" by Tammi Knorr

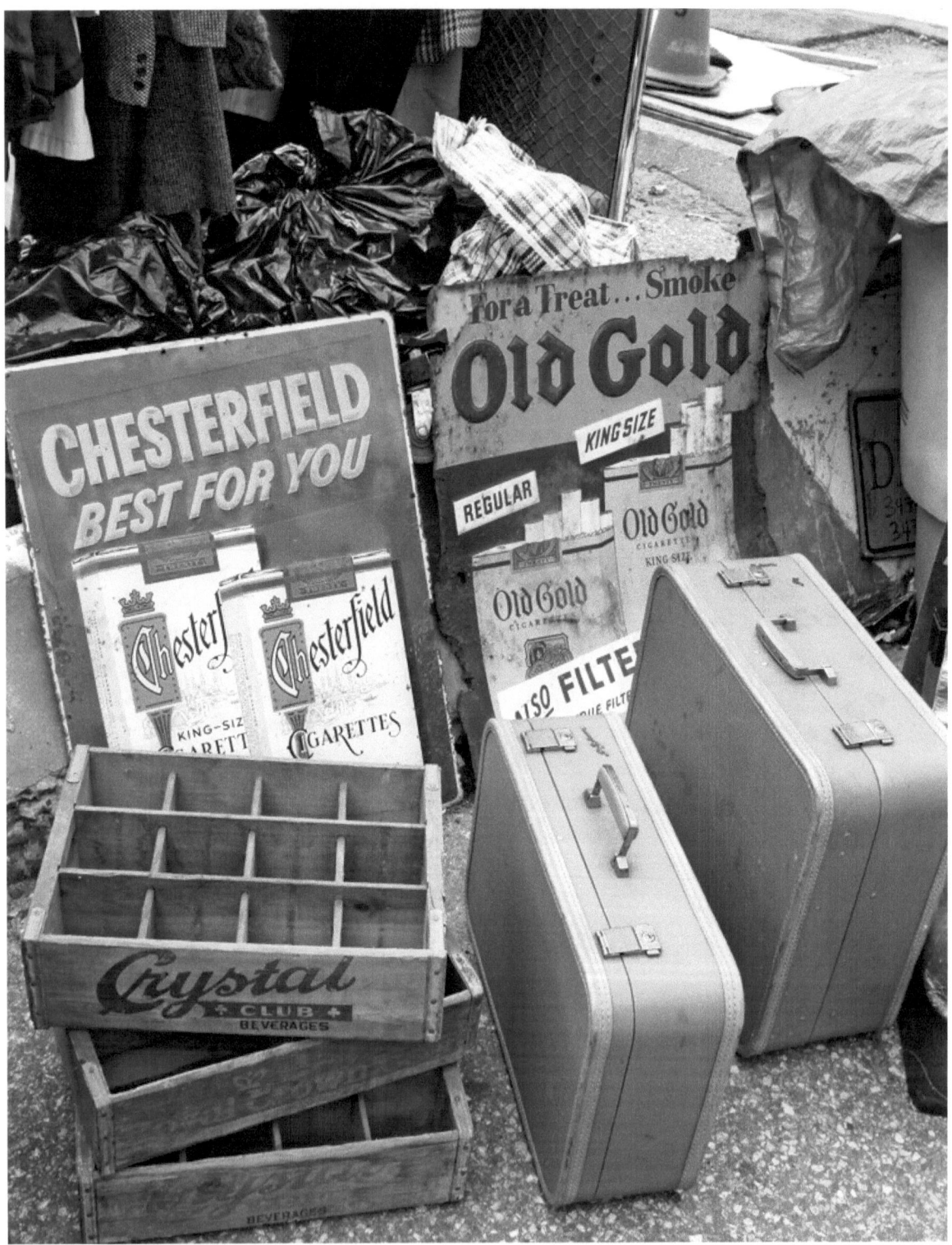

"Old Gold" by Lawrence von Knorr

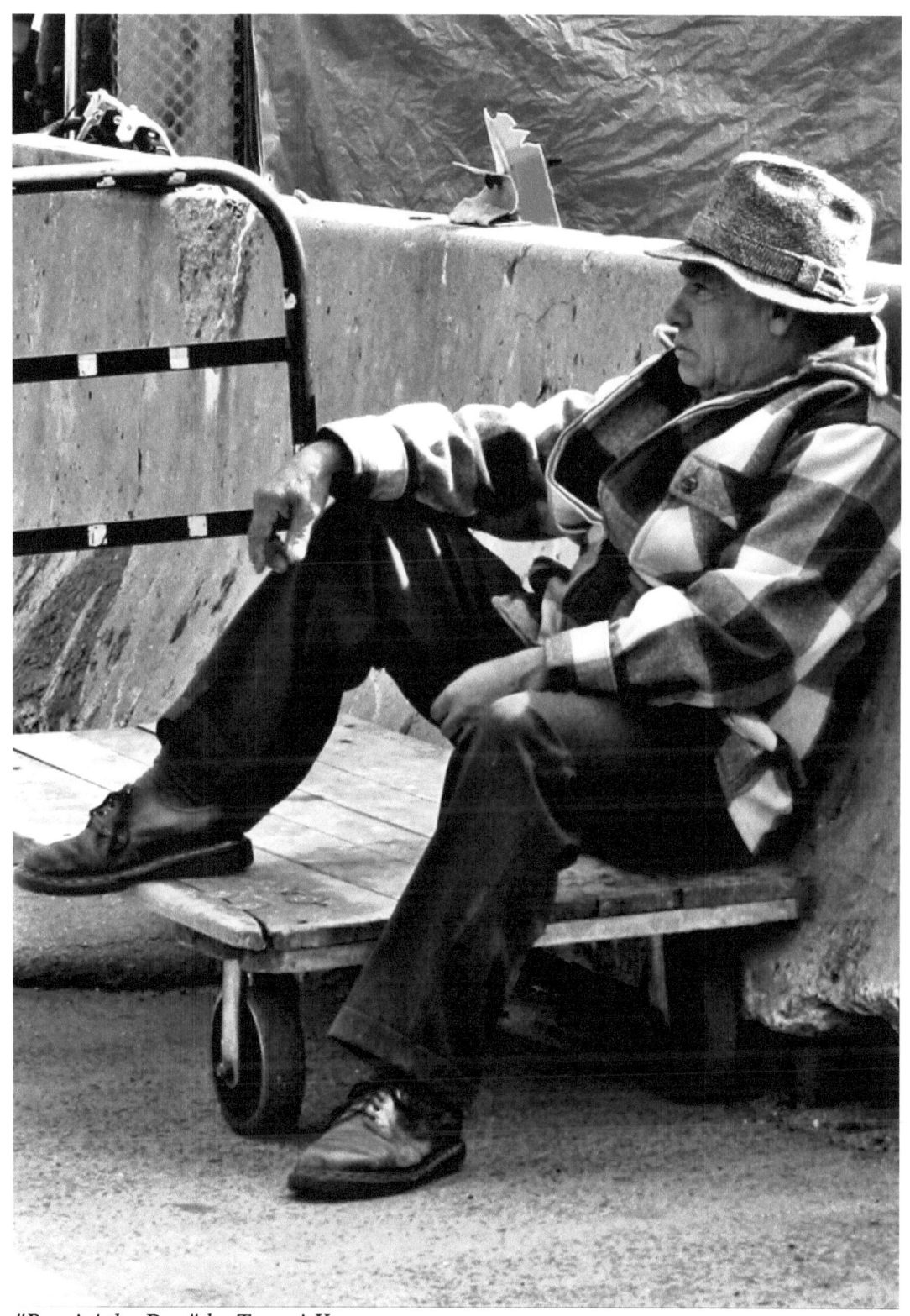

"Passin' the Day" by Tammi Knorr

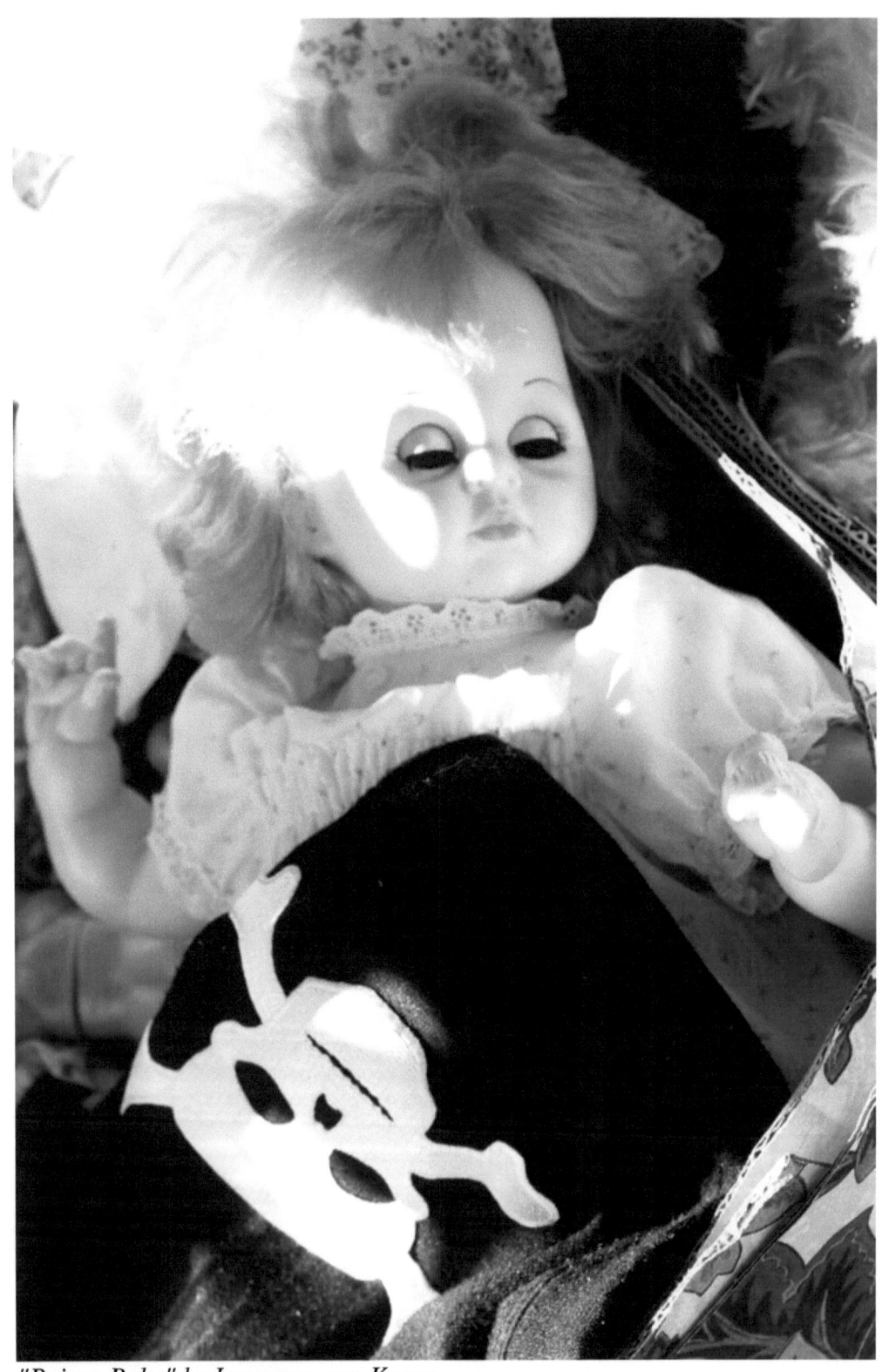
"Poison Baby" by Lawrence von Knorr

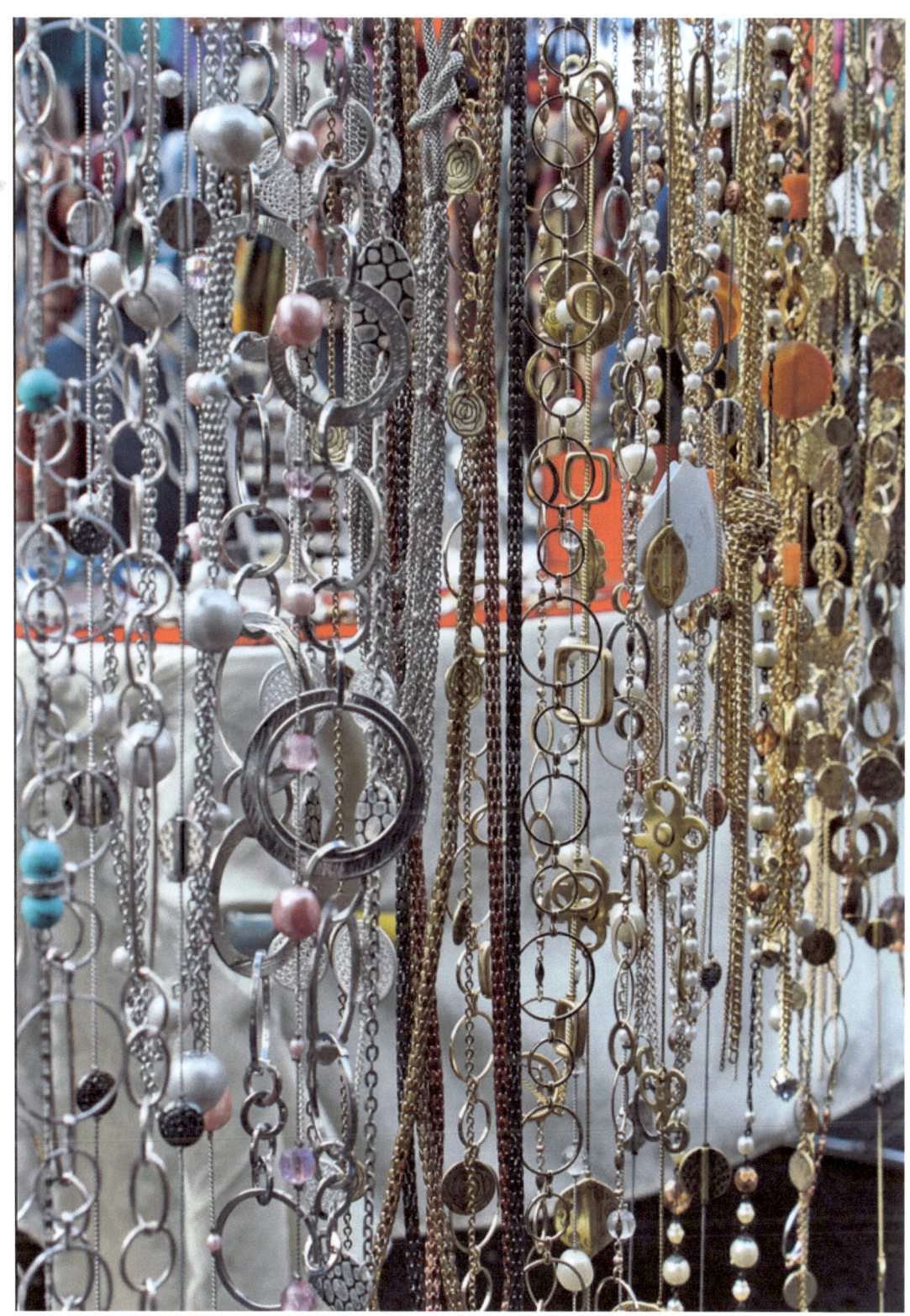

"Precious Metal" by Tammi Knorr

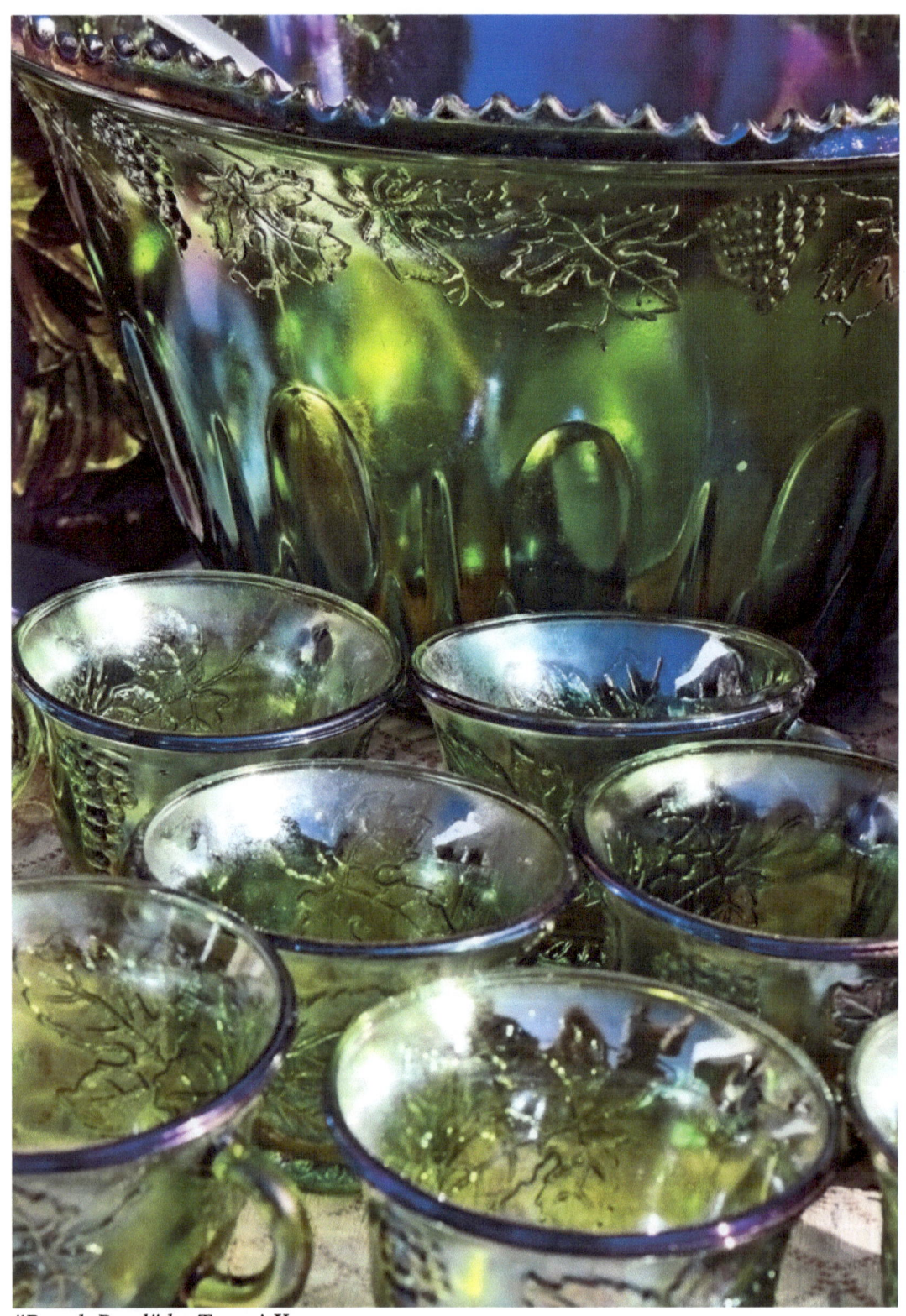

"Punch Bowl" by Tammi Knorr

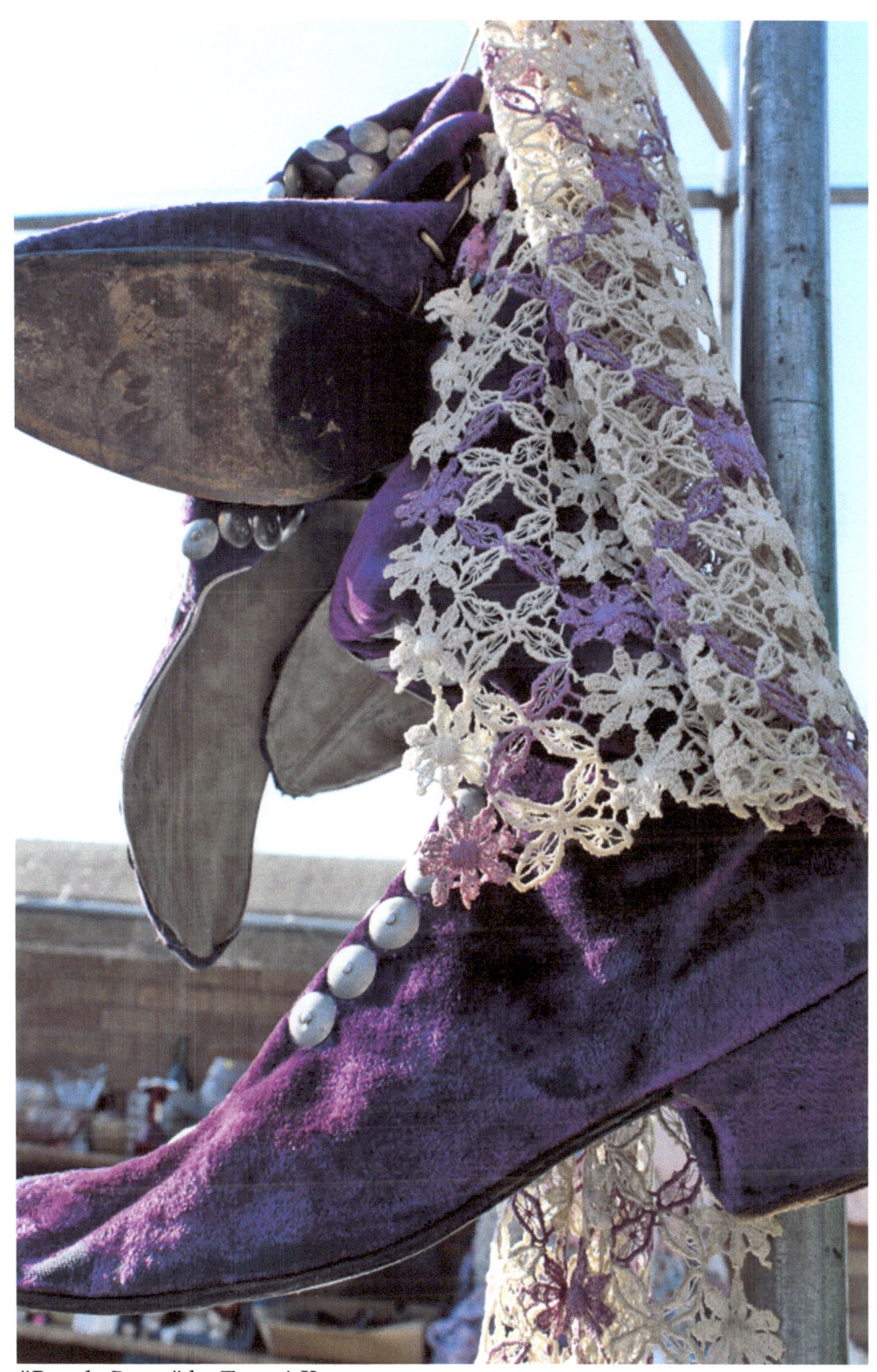

"Purple Boots" by Tammi Knorr

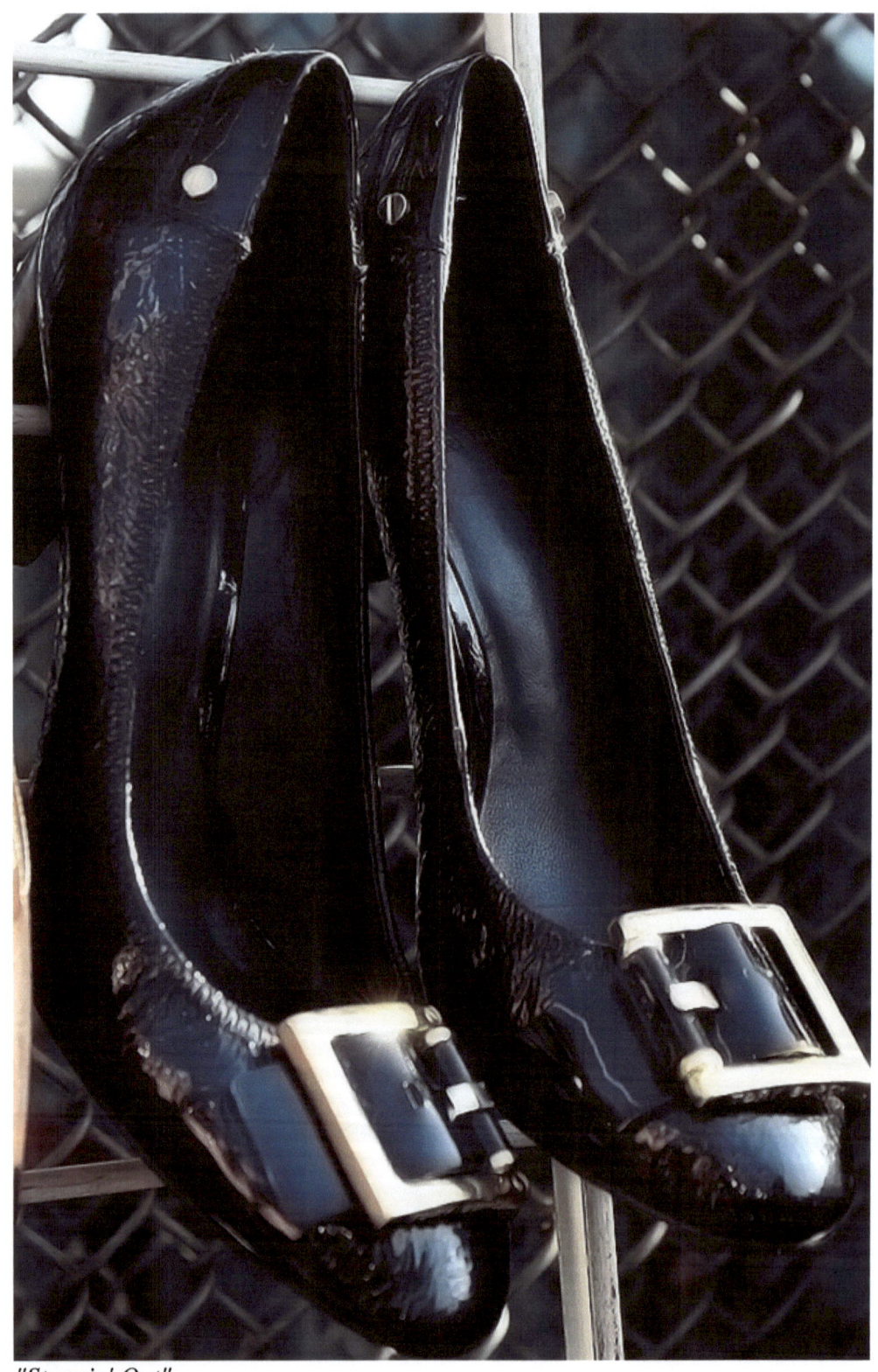

"Steppin' Out"

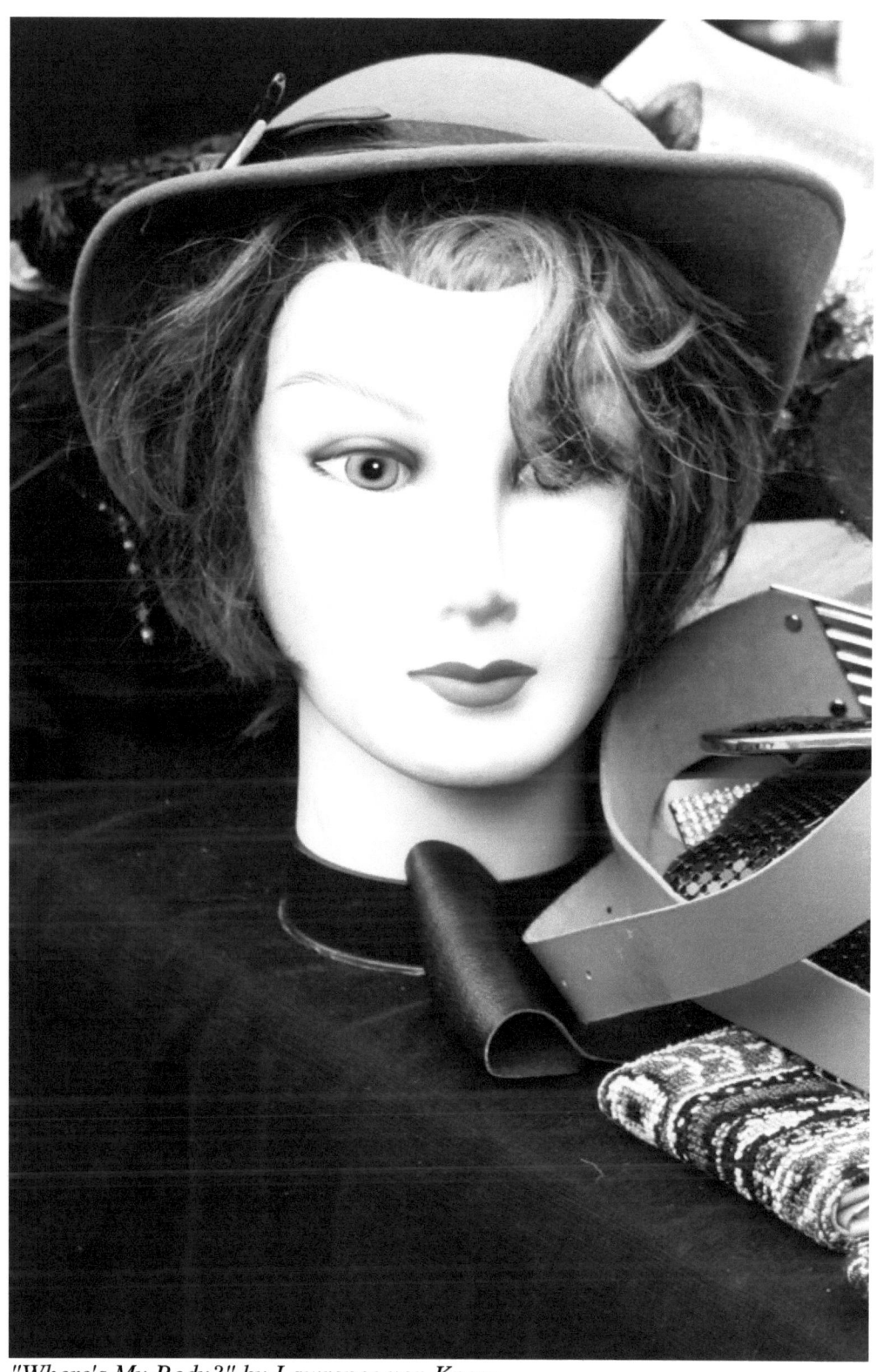

"Where's My Body?" by Lawrence von Knorr

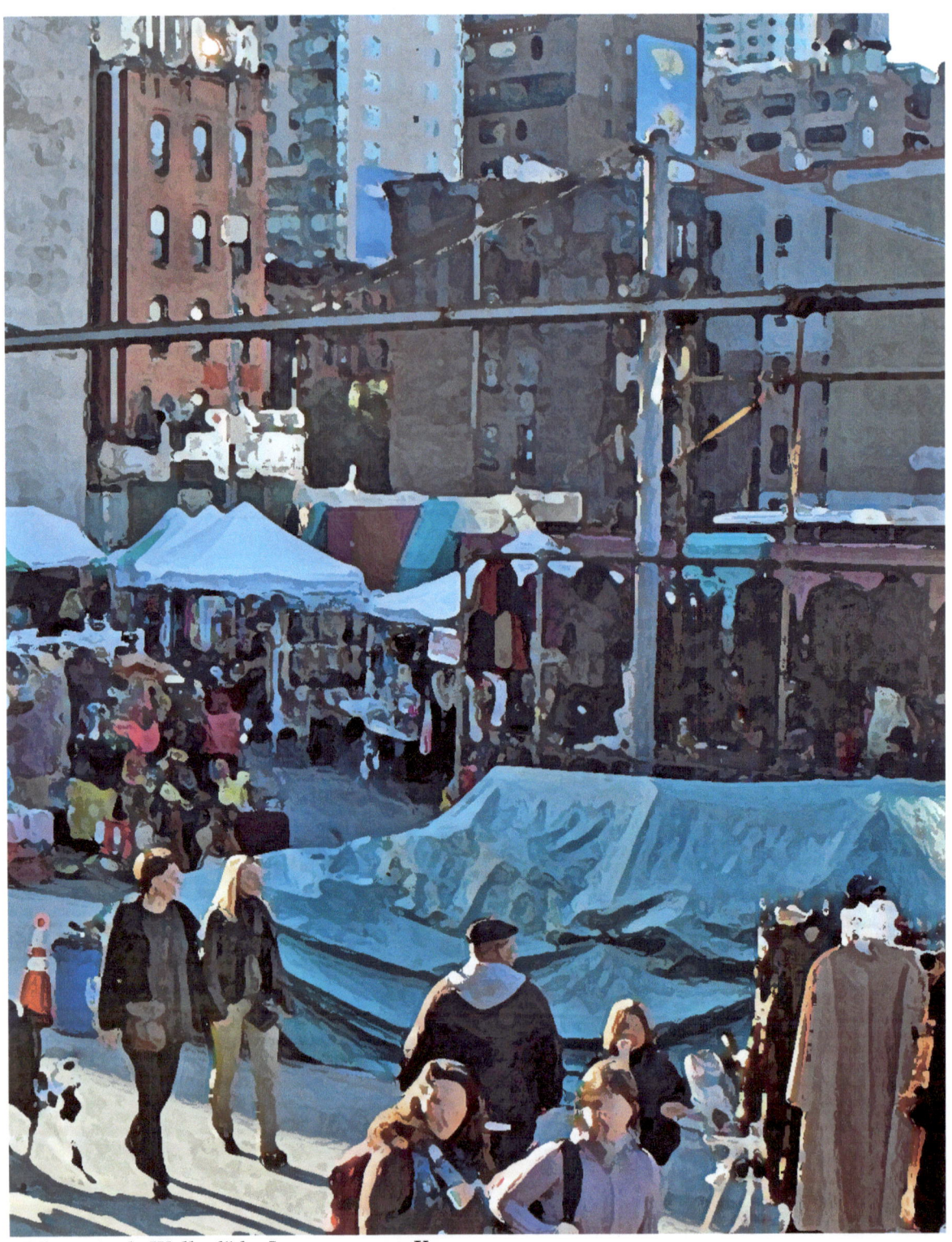
"Where Andy Walked" by Lawrence von Knorr

www.ingramcontent.com/pod-product-compliance
Lightning Source LLC
Chambersburg PA
CBHW051219220526
45473CB00003B/1099